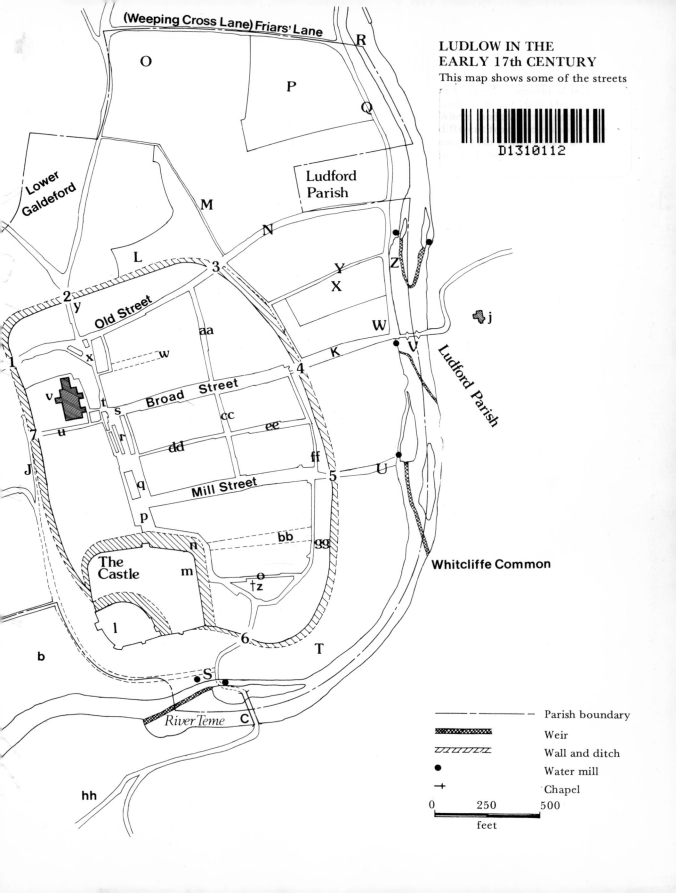

(Weeping Cross Lane) Friars' Lane

O

P

R

Q

**LUDLOW IN THE EARLY 17th CENTURY**
This map shows some of the streets

D1310112

Lower
Galdeford

M

Ludford
Parish

N

L

Y

X

Z

3

2

y

Old Street

W

j

aa

K

4

x

w

Broad    Street

V

Ludford Parish

1

v

t    s

cc

ee

7

u

r

dd

ff

J

q

5

U

Mill Street

p

bb

gg

Whitcliffe Common

n

The
Castle

m

o

†z

l

6

T

b

S

River Teme

C

hh

Parish boundary

Weir

Wall and ditch

● Water mill

† Chapel

0    250    500
feet

To Wendy and Valerie

*In amoris causa*

# LUDLOW
## A Historic Town in Words and Pictures

# FRONTISPIECE

This print was published in 1811 as the frontispiece to William Felton's *Description of the Town of Ludlow*, one of the best of the early guidebooks. The painter was William Gwynn, a local artist, and it is tempting to think that the young man who is sketching may be a self-portrait. The view was taken from Hill Close on Gravel Hill, near the site of the present East Hamlet Hospital, and is looking south west.

The picture emphasises the twin foci of the historic town: the Castle and the Parish Church. They stand on the crest of the hill or *low* which is the suffix of the place-name *Ludlow*. The rapids or *loud waters* which provide the prefix *lud* are not visible from this angle but the steep slopes of the gorge of the River Teme, where the rapids occur, can be seen rising up to the Castle. Though masked by trees the long line of Corve Street, where Gwynn himself lived, can be seen in the middle distance, climbing towards the church.

Beyond the town is the broad expanse of Whitcliffe, common land since the 13th century. The upper parts had recently been lost to large fields enclosed by straight hedges, a striking feature on the picture, but the lower slopes remained for recreation and sheep grazing and are still a valued public amenity in 1984.

The slopes of Whitcliffe and those of Hill Close, which rise out of the picture towards Titterstone Clee Hill, form a broad valley in which the smaller *hill by the rapids* is situated. Since prehistoric times this valley has been followed by important routes, e.g. the *Principal Road* mapped by John Ogilby in 1675, the A49 and the Chester-Cardiff railway of today. Control of this routeway has brought the town much of its strategic importance through the ages.

The foreground of the picture has been over-run by late 19th and 20th century housing but the distant view from this position in 1984 is little different from that of 1811.

# Ludlow

## A Historic Town
## in Words and Pictures

## David Lloyd & Peter Klein

## Phillimore

1984

Published by
PHILLIMORE & CO. LTD.,
Shopwyke Hall, Chichester, Sussex

ISBN 0 85033 514 0

Printed and bound in Great Britain by
BILLING & SONS LTD.
Worcester, England

# LIST OF CONTENTS AND ILLUSTRATIONS

# PREFACE

Ludlow is a small market town in the south of Shropshire, a few miles east of the Welsh border. Its population today is about 7,700 but until the late 18th century it rarely had more than 2,000 inhabitants. The town is not mentioned in the Domesday Book but a castle was started on the site between 1086 and 1094 and by 1138 or earlier the place name 'Lodelowe' was in use.

L. Braithwaite in *The Historic Towns of Britain* asserts that 'for many people Ludlow is the perfect historic town'. It is often cited as a classic example of a Norman planned town which preserves much of its 12th-century rectilinear plan; while many of the medieval burgage plots remain intact and can be studied on the ground. There are 469 listed buildings, i.e. one to every 16 inhabitants, a higher ratio than in almost any other historic town.

The buildings and other visual evidence, e.g. the tombs in the Parish Church, mirror the principal phases of the town's development. In the Middle Ages Ludlow was an important centre for the collection and sale of wool and for the manufacture of cloth. Ludlow merchants traded in the Low Countries while broadcloths called 'Ludlow whytes' fetched good prices in London. In the late 15th century the Castle became the headquarters of the Council of the Marches and for the next 200 years Ludlow was virtually the capital of Wales and the border counties. Judges, lawyers and civil servants lived in the town and there was 'great access of straungers'. The Council was abolished in 1689, when the new government wished to centralise authority in London, but local gentry and nobility continued to spend part of each year in Ludlow. This helped the town to develop as a fashionable social centre and the resulting prosperity lasted until the mid-19th century, when improved communications enabled the leisured classes to travel elsewhere. In Victorian times the town was less prosperous though the growth of residential suburbs to the east, on what had been part of the town fields, helped to relieve overcrowding in the town centre.

This book introduces the history of Ludlow by a chronological sequence of descriptions and illustrations. Many of the descriptions were written by visitors to the town but others are the work of chroniclers and historians or are taken from local guidebooks, letters and newspapers or from works of literature associated with Ludlow. The book is intended as an introduction to a definitive history of the town which is being prepared by the Ludlow Historical Research Group, using a wide range of documentary sources and evidence of the town plan and standing buildings.

Inevitably such a book has two kinds of bias. First, source material is more abundant for the later centuries than for the Middle Ages, particularly with regard to illustrations. The earliest-known pictures of Ludlow are as late as 1684, though visual material of other kinds is available, e.g. the wood carvings and stained glass windows of the parish church. Second, such a collection is biased in favour of the impressive and the extra-ordinary at the expense of the commonplace. From the 12th century to the 20th most descriptions of the town highlight the Castle and ignore such streets as Holdgate Fee and Lower Galdeford. Again, the difference is most apparent in illustrations. Even in the 19th-century pictures of the Castle, the church, Broad Street and the *Feathers* are plentiful while those of less fashionable parts of the town are very rare or non-existent. Every attempt has been made to correct the first imbalance by the occasional inclusion of other types of historical document, e.g. a probate inventory of 1661 and a list of those receiving poor relief in 1817. The major corrective, however, will come in later publications and it is hoped that this book will be seen as part of a series rather than in isolation.

Nevertheless, the material chosen does provide an informative and at times entertaining commentary on nine centuries of Ludlow history. Most of the written extracts are already in print but often in rare and not easily-accessible publications. There have, of course, been agonies of selection, especially for the later centuries, and other historians faced with the same sources may well have chosen differently. Having made their choice the authors can only share the hope of John Price, who wrote the first edition of *A Ludlow Guide* in 1795, that 'it may meet the approbation and patronage of the Public'.

# ACKNOWLEDGEMENTS

Since the Ludlow Historical Research Group was formed in 1976 there has been increasing enthusiasm for local history in and around Ludlow, reminiscent of the interest in geology which accompanied the foundation of Ludlow Natural History and its museum in 1833. This book owes much to the interest and goodwill of many people. Many unknown illustrations and documents have come to light in this way and the attention of the authors has been drawn to rare and little known sources of information.

More specific acknowledgement must be made to the patient and painstaking work of members of the Research Group over the last eight years. Much of this will bear full fruit in the material to be presented in later volumes but some of the information in this book could only have come to light through the systematic transcription and processing of a range of historical documents. In 1983-4 there are 38 subscribing members but many others have participated in former years. Thanks must also go to the members of the Birmingham University Extra Mural classes on the history of Ludlow over the past five years. The lively discussions held with this group have been a stimulating testing ground for many interpretations of Ludlow's history.

Very special thanks are due to Michael Faraday, who works in London and thus had opportunity to transcribe and process all the Ludlow material in the Public Record Office. As an expert medievalist he has also worked on a range of other documents and has kindly undertaken all the Latin-English translations required for this book. Thanks are also due to Harry Baker, who has taken a keen interest in this publication and has supplied several important references, including the extract from the work on Walter White which is quoted on pages 102-3. We also thank Christine Upton, who did much of the preliminary research on the Fitzwarine Romance; Margaret Richards, who researched the information on costumes presented on pages 24-5; Geoffrey and Nancy Cox, who made useful comments on the inventory reproduced on page 50; and Madge Moran, who has always been our architectural consultant, though buildings are not the main focus of this book.

We gladly acknowledge the co-operation received from the staffs of many libraries and record offices. Active research on our behalf by Tony Carr and his colleagues at the Shropshire Local Studies Library is especially appreciated. As for all work on Ludlow much is owed to Marion Halford of the Shropshire Record Office and to Sue Hubbard of the Herefordshire Record Office and to their assistants. The staff of the History, Literature and Local Studies departments of Birmingham City Library have been especially helpful in tracking down obscure references. In Ludlow John Norton and Howard Cheese have generously put the records and illustrations of the Museum at our disposal and have also helped in other ways.

Thanks are due to Dr. Barrie Trinder, who first put us in touch with Phillimore & Co. and to Noel Osborne, Phillimore's Editorial Director, who encouraged and commissioned this work. A book of this nature needs considerable care with layout and design and we are grateful to Dr. Frances Condick and Frances Mee for their patience and skill and to everyone else at Phillimore involved in this project. Finally, we acknowledge gratefully the services of Gillian Bradley of Tenbury Wells, who has drawn most of the maps and annotated diagrams.

We would also like to thank the following persons and institutions for help with illustrations and/or for their permission to reproduce material in their possession: Direct Designs, Alvechurch, for no. 1; Gillian Bradley for nos. 2, 4, 33, 36, 38, 52 and 78; Aerofilms (Boreham Wood) for no. 5; the Bodleian Library, Oxford, for no. 7; the Francis Frith Postcard Collection for nos. 9, 12 and 14; Michael Davighi for no. 13; the Shropshire Local Studies Library for nos. 40, 47, 49, 73, 74, 110 and 168; Annette Roe and the Birmingham University Archaeological Field Unit for no. 41; the Shropshire Archaeological Society for nos. 44 and 45; Harry Field for no. 59; the Ordnance Survey (Crown Copyright Reserved) for nos. 71, 90 and 118; the University of Birmingham for nos. 75 and 76; Ludlow Museum for nos. 77, 79, 80, 81, 119, 154 and 156; the Public Record Office for no. 82; the British Library for nos. 83 and 112; Messrs. Spinks for no. 84; the Henry E. Huntington Library and Art Gallery, San Marino, U.S.A., for no. 86; Mr. and Mrs. L. Darton of Ludlow for no. 87; the Victoria and Albert Museum for no. 98; Dr. M. Speight for no. 126; Messrs. Christie for no. 139; Birmingham City Library for nos. 140-142; Peter Bartlett for no. 152; Margaret Green for nos. 163 and 164; and Stanley Woolston for no. 170. Nos. 6, 10, 11, 15-28 inclusive, 31, 32, 34, 35, 37, 39, 46, 48, 50, 60, 88, 91, 104, 108, 109, 149 and 153 were photographed by Peter Klein and no. 169 by David Lloyd.

# INTRODUCTION

Relative to other towns, Ludlow was more important in the Middle Ages than at any other time in its history. In 1377 it had a tax paying population of 1,172 and ranked as the 33rd largest provincial town in England, ahead of Derby, Lichfield and Southampton, though barely half the size of Shrewsbury and Hereford.[1] Some of this importance was due to the lords of the Castle, especially the Lacys and the Mortimers, who became embroiled in national politics; but more fundamentally it reflected its economic prosperity based on the collection and sale of wool and on the manufacture of cloth. In the 13th and 14th centuries particularly Ludlow merchants attained great wealth and influence; in 1355, for instance, William de Orleton, 'merchant of Lodelowe', lent £120 to the Black Prince.[2] The Parish Church, largely rebuilt between 1433 and 1471, is one of the largest in England and eloquently reflects the town's medieval status.

The town's importance brought many visitors to Ludlow, some of them men of national standing. In 1225 Stephen Langton, Archbishop of Canterbury, was in attendance at the Castle when William Marshall, Earl of Pembroke, treated on the King's behalf with Llewellyn the Great, the rebel Welsh prince.[3] In the 1450s Richard Plantagenet, Duke of York, was Lord of Ludlow and also leader of the Yorkist faction and thus important allies like the Nevilles were often in and out of the town. Travellers further down the social scale were accommodated at the town's inns, some of which still retain medieval features, e.g. the long back range at the *Bull*, where each bay has a stable below and a first floor open hall above. Many travelling craftsmen visited the town, e.g. the mason of Gloucester and his man who were given a 'dyn' worth 6d when they came to Ludlow in 1469 to advise on the construction of the church tower.[4] In spite of the difficulties of medieval travel there was frequent contact between Ludlow and the major centres of population. A scandal of 1423, which is recorded in the rolls of the King's Bench, is one of many such instances. David Chirbury (d.1456), Prior of the Carmelite Friary in Corve Street and later Bishop of Dromore, was frequently in London. Whilst there he 'abducted in his service' Hugh Money, son of William Money, tailor. This led to William Money, Thomas William of London, armourer, and others journeying to Ludlow, where they broke into the Prior's Close and released young Hugh 'with force and arms'.[5]

In spite of these comings and goings very few descriptions of medieval Ludlow have survived. If accounts were written there was no means of printing them until the very end of the period; while as manuscripts they were less likely to be preserved than leases, wills, court rolls and other documents of legal validity. The Domesday Book of 1086 gives detailed information on the ancient parish of Stanton Lacy but there is no reference to the future site of Ludlow. Monastic and other chroniclers, in their surveys of national history, refer to the town when it became involved in major political events. Such instances occurred in 1138 and 1139 when the *castellum de Ludelowe* was held by a rival baron and attacked by King Stephen himself. This incident is described by no less than eight monastic chroniclers, though some of them wrote many years after the event. Later political events are also described by chroniclers, e.g. the rise and fall of Roger Mortimer in the 1320s and the sacking of Ludlow by the Lancastrians in 1459. Only rarely are economic and social matters related by the chroniclers, an exception being the career of the great wool merchant Laurence de Ludlow (d. 1294), a figure of national standing.

The only travel writer known to have visited Ludlow in the Middle Ages is Giraldus Cambrensis in 1188 but his description of the Castle is very brief. The most interesting descriptions of medieval Ludlow are those contained in the delightful but enigmatic Fitzwarine Romance, an early 14th-century prose tale in Anglo-Norman French which deals with events supposedly set in the first half of the 12th century. Scholars working on this important document agree that the author was a Ludlovian who was at his best when 'on home ground writing about Ludlow Castle'; but some of his topographical details cannot be located with certainty.

Medieval illustrations of towns are extremely rare, though important details were sometimes included incidentally in pictures of other subjects, e.g. the 'hypothetical but typical medieval town' which can be glimpsed through the window in 'The Virgin and Child before a Fire-Screen' by the Dutch painter Robert Campin (1378-1444).[6] No such illustrations have survived for Ludlow but the wood carvings and stained glass windows in the Parish Church, though often of conventional designs, give important details of contemporary costumes and of domestic and working life. Other details of the economy have been taken from the borough charter of 1461, which has been in print since 1821.

In the 16th and 17th centuries Ludlow became an important administrative town. The Council of the Marches of Wales had its headquarters at Ludlow Castle and the town was virtually the capital of the principality and the border counties. The Council had its roots in the small group of courtiers attending Prince Edward, son of King Edward IV, who was sent to live at Ludlow Castle between 1473 and 1483; but it lacked real authority until the 1530s when a newly-appointed Lord President, Bishop Rowland Lee, ruthlessly enforced the law and made 'all Wales quake with feare'. The effects of the Council on the local economy are complex and will be considered in detail in the next volume; but contemporary observers agree that there was 'great access of straungers'. It is no coincidence that 10 of the 13 passages covering the 1536-1689 period are concerned with the Council of the Marches in some way.

John Leland, 'that tireless travelling antiquary' who visited Ludlow in the early 1540s, makes no reference to the Council and both he and John Ogilby, who published an atlas of 100 road maps in 1675, would have come to Ludlow even if it had not been the Council's headquarters. Equally, it is certain that some reference to the town would have been made in William Camden's comprehensive *Brittania* (published in 1587) with or without the Council's presence, though he includes interesting material on the latter at the end of his account. On the other hand the Shrewsbury poet Thomas Churchyard gives it special prominence. In *The Worthiness of Wales*, published in the same year as *Brittania*, he devotes 250 lines to Ludlow because, he says, 'it stands for Wales, most apt, most fit and best'. Many of Ludlow's visitors were litigants from all parts of Wales and the border counties but most of those of high rank came from England, e.g. the 'Earle of Essex' in 1584-85 when 'iijs.iiijd.' was 'geven to the Ringers' of the parish church bells.[7] No written descriptions survive, however, until 1684, five years before the abolition of the Council, when Henry, Duke of Beaufort, the last but one Lord President, made an official Progress through Wales and the border counties. He was accompanied by Thomas Dineley, a Herefordshire gentleman, who wrote a detailed account of things which he saw and also made drawings. Apart from thumb-nail sketches of Ludford Bridge and the remnants of St John's Hospital, made in the corner of a map in 1577, Dineley's drawings are the earliest extant pictures of Ludlow and give a particularly fine portrayal of the Castle during its last years of habitation.

In spite of distance and the poor condition of the roads, Ludlow was no provincial backwater during these years. Messengers using post horses could come from London in less than two days. Queen Elizabeth died late on 24 March 1602/3 but James I was proclaimed in Ludlow at noon on 26 March 1603.[8] Large collections of official letters survive, many of them abstracted in printed calendars. Most of these letters are principally concerned with administrative details but some give insights into the thoughts of their writers and into local conditions. On 21 August 1602, for example, Lord Zouch (1556-1625), recently appointed Lord President, complained to Sir Robert Cecil, the Queen's chief minister, that he need been sent 'to a place where he deserves not to settle', and also revealed that the harvest 'is very backward and full of wet'.[9] One such letter, written by Lord President Rowland Lee in 1534, has been included, and also a selection from the letters of Lady Brilliana Harley, the wife of a Councillor, written just before and during the 1642-46 Civil War.

The intelligentsia of this time was a comparatively small circle and links between the mini-court at Ludlow and the mainstream of national culture were commonplace. Sir Philip Sidney, who made a major contribution to Renaissance literature, was the son of the best-known Lord President, though his association with Ludlow is often exaggerated. Richard Baxter, later a famous Presbyterian divine, was sent to Ludlow Castle in 1631 as a private pupil of the Chaplain to the Council, instead of going to university, though he found 'many idle gentlemen' at the castle and the town 'full of temptations'. Samuel Butler (1612-80), author of *Hudibras*, was a secretary at the castle for a short time after the Restoration and may have written part of that work whilst in residence there.[10] The castle certainly had a cultural life of its own and bands of travelling actors often performed there, e.g. 'my lord Staffordes players in the Ester weeke that played in the Castill' in 1576.[11] Masques and other entertainments were often presented but it was a series of chances that led to the most famous first performance at Ludlow on Michaelmas night 1634, of the masque by John Milton which was later known as *Comus*. Although it tells us little about Ludlow itself, a section on *Comus* has been included in this book, but there is no room for the satirical wit of *Hudibras*, much of which is meaningless to 20th-century readers. More bizarre literary links can sometimes be detected, e.g. with John Hall (1575-1636) of Stratford, Shakespeare's son-in-law, who was a fashionable society doctor. Hall came to Ludlow nine times between 1617 and 1630 to attend the Countess of Northampton, wife of the Lord President, who was suffering from dropsy.[12] It is reported that in 1620 he treated her with such a violent purge that she passed 41 stools in three days but within 20 days was cured. Such anecdotes are the spice of history and they occur more frequently for Ludlow because of the presence there of the Council of the Marches.

The lack of illustrations of Ludlow before 1684 is as surprising as it is disappointing. The Welsh border, it is true, was outside the circuit of fashionable artists like Hendrick Danckerts (c.1630-80), who came from the Netherlands to draw English palaces;[13] but the importance of the Castle was such that some pictures must have been made. It is disappointing, also, that Celia Fiennes (1662-1741), one of the most informative and entertaining of travel writers, never came to Ludlow. She visited Shrewsbury in 1698, finding it 'a pleasant town to live in', but then made a great loop to the east through Kidderminster and Worcester to Bristol.[14]

There is ample compensation, however, in the exceptionally fine panoramic view of the town painted in 1722, which is reproduced on the jacket of this book and on pages 62-65. It was produced for a local patron by another Dutchman, Isaac Vogelsanck, and the court miniaturist, Bernard Lens. The period 1719-22 was indeed a remarkably rich one for both written and visual material. Joseph Smith's interesting—but inaccurate—picture of the town was published in 1719, as was the first known Ludlow newspaper, while visitors during the next three years included the perceptive antiquarian William Stukeley and the diarist and novelist Daniel Defoe. The first quarter of the 18th century also saw the (unpublished) work of Edward Lloyd, arguably Shropshire's first documentary historian, while a few years later the Rev. William Mytton visited the town and made over one hundred drawings of monuments and coats of arms. This flurry of activity is in contrast to the 1735-65 period which produced no descriptions or pictures worth including in this book.

The half century after 1765 is another richly-rewarding period. Ludlow was then thriving as a fashionable social centre while the improved roads of the First and Second Ludlow Turnpike Trusts, founded in 1751 and 1756, brought an increasing number of visitors, especially after 1791, when the war with France precluded the traditional 'grand tour' of Europe. Though the majority of inhabitants lived a life of drudgery and discomfort, the town of these years was a lesser version of Bath. In 1810, indeed, it was seriously proposed that cheap local fuel should be used to provide 'warm and hot baths' and that a crescent of houses should be built on Whitcliffe.[15]

Well-known landscape painters visited the town, including Samuel Scott, William Marlow and J. M. W. Turner. These painters were all attracted by the 'picturesque' ruined castle but it was only Samuel Scott, who resided in Broad Street for three years before gout drove him to Bath itself, who painted other parts of the town. Like other social centres the town produced its own local artists, including William Owen who became Principal Portrait Painter to the Prince Regent. William Gwynn of Corve Street also achieved some London success but spent most of his life in Ludlow. Beginning in 1794 there was a spate of local histories and guidebooks, most of which were illustrated by local artists. The earliest guidebook was written by an impecunious schoolmaster, John Price of Leominster, but such enterprises were promoted by the local booksellers, especially Henry Proctor of Broad Street and William Felton of King Street. The town produced other sorts of local writers, ranging in quality from the doggerel verse of Joseph Bullock to the delightful girlhood memories of Mary Sneade, some of which were published in Carola Oman's *Ayot Rectory* in 1965.

The turnpike roads and the improvements in coach services also brought diarists and travel writers, many of them 'en route' to or from picturesque North Wales. Travel guides and books on antiquities were published to meet the needs of such travellers and there are at least 15 printed descriptions of Ludlow between 1769 and 1818, excluding books of purely local interest. Most of these eulogise Ludlow though a few censorious comments are included. A tourist of 1772 found provisions 'cheap' and the company 'very good' while he had also seen 'abundance of pretty ladies here'.[16] In 1797 *The Gentleman's Magazine* called Ludlow 'one of the handsomest country towns in England' while in 1798 *The Modern Universal British Traveller* found 'the houses well built and the streets exceeding clean' and noted that 'many people of rank and fortune constantly reside in it'.[17] The following year, however, George Lipscomb, on his *Journey into South Wales* found 'an air of quietness which the size of the town rendered unexpected' and concluded that 'dulness seems, indeed, to have established her reign here'.[18] The works of two visitors, John Byng in 1784 and William Mavor in 1803, have been selected to represent this rash of travel writing.

The 19th century produced so much descriptive writing on Ludlow that there is no room in this selection for an author of the eminence of Henry James, who visited the town in 1870 and found in its 'wide streets' evidence that it had once been 'the centre of a large, provincial society'.[19] The 'Reminiscences of an Old Inhabitant', written in 1905, is the best of several pieces written by local residents while visitors as diverse as a Bewdley corn merchant, an American tourist and the Librarian of the Royal Society all make pertinent comments on the town. A different kind of visitor was the Edinburgh cartographer, John Wood, who published a map of Ludlow in 1835. Thomas Wright, senior, in 1822, John Evans in 1861 and Oliver Baker in 1888 produced what are arguably the best of many local guidebooks. Thomas Wright, junior, whose *History of Ludlow* was published in two parts in 1841 and 1843, and Henry Weyman, who wrote on many aspects of Ludlow round the turn of the century, represent a growing body of local historians. County historians who worked on Ludlow included the Rev. R. W. Eyton, whose massive *Antiquities of Shropshire* was published in 1859, and the Rev. D. H. S. Cranage, whose *An Architectural Account of the Churches of Shropshire*, published in 1895, remains the definitive work. Two poems only can represent the work of A. E. Housman and there is room for just one extract from the historical novelist Stanley Weyman, a member of a well-known Ludlow family. A letter from *The Ludlow Advertiser* of 1862 is informative and entertaining enough to displace the macabre details of an attempted murder at the *Angel*, published in the short-lived *Ludlow Standard* in 1840.

The visual records of these years are also plentiful though the Castle, the church, Broad Street and the *Feathers* are consistently the most popular subjects, at the expense of less fashionable parts of the town. Work by William Gwynn covers the first six decades of the century while nationally-known artists Henry Ziegler and Louise Rayner produced high quality work on Ludlow. Topographical artists were progressively superceded by the development of photography after 1860. Francis Bedford and Benjamin Stone were photographers of wide repute who worked in Ludlow after 1860 but some of the most pleasing shots were produced by Broad Street photographer Thomas Jones and by a number of local amateurs. Volumes of Ludlow views were published by Ludlow booksellers, e.g. W. Partridge and J. C. Austen, while advertisements in trade directories and newspapers provide other forms of visual illustrations.

In the 20th century the lower cost of printing has brought an explosion of printing and permitted the development of the popular craze for topographical postcards. Both national firms and local shops published series of local views. A new type of travel book accompanied the popularisation of the motor car, just as earlier publications had marked the coaching era. Thirty-five books mentioning Ludlow between 1900 and 1940 have been identified, e.g. *Picturesque Towns and Villages* published by Edward Burrow for Dunlop in 1928. Ludlow is described as 'standing magnificently upon its hill', while there is reference to 'the ruined castle', 'the many ancient houses' and 'the parish church with its ancient woodwork, glass and monuments'. Batsford Ltd. were one of the firms specialising in this kind of literature and their inter-war lists included H. Ebertein's *Little Known England* (1930), C. B. Ford's *Landscape of England* (1933) and C. Rouse's *The Old Towns of England* (1936), all of which contain somewhat over-romanticised descriptions of Ludlow.

•In the years after the Second World War there has been a further increase in topographical literature. Some of this is of mediocre quality but high standards have been reached both in architectural appreciation and in historical analysis. Christopher Hussey, who wrote four articles on Ludlow in *Country Life* in 1945 and 1946, won the vote for inclusion in this book by a short head over Nikolaus Pevsner and Alec Clifton-Taylor. Pevsner, in the *Shropshire* volume of the Buildings of England series, illustrates his gift for the memorable phrase, e.g. the 'arrogantly high tower' of the parish church; of the 'painful jog' of Lloyds Bank; but he is at his most perceptive when writing about the infilling of the ancient High Street.[20] The town, he says, 'as one wanders through it, has a narrow and a spacious part . . . Both are needed in a town and may Ludlow never decide to pull down its tortuous centre to please the gentleman motorist or the charabanc tourist'. Clifton-Taylor, in *Six English Towns* (1978) is equally out-spoken but he is full of praise for the town's fabric for 'here at Ludlow we find a delightful mixture of building materials, all of local provenance'.[21] As all these writers imply, the town's aesthetic qualities are closely linked with its historical evolution, the understanding of which has been transformed by the school of townscape historians who owe allegiance to Professor W. G. Hoskins. Pages 123-25 give a hint of what can be achieved by these techniques and of what will be presented in later volumes of this series. The extract chosen for inclusion on page 122 is that by William St John Hope on 'The Ancient Topography of the Town of Ludlow'; though published in 1909 this article has been the starting point for all serious work on the town plan in the post-war years.

The greatest contribution to the more traditional documentary type of history has been made by the second and third volumes of the *Victoria County History*. Volume 2, published in 1973, contains authoritative articles on the Palmers' Guild, the town's religious houses, Hosier's Almshouses and the Grammar School, all written by the dedicated editor, Alec Gaydon. The third volume, edited by his successor George Baugh, was published in 1979 and has important articles on the town's Parliamentary representation and on other aspects of local government.

## NOTES

1. Hoskins, W. G., *Local History in England* (2nd edn., 1972), p. 238.
2. The Black Prince's Register.
3. Weyman, 1911, pp. 15-16.
4. Jones, L., *Church Wardens' accounts of the Town of Ludlow* (1892), p. 8.
5. P.R.O., K.B.27/652, m.65r.
6. Jacobs, D., *Master Builders of the Middle Ages* (1970), p. 43.
7. SRO 356 box 472, Church.Wardens' Accounts, 1584/5. We are grateful to John Lamb of L.H.R.G. for drawing our attention to this reference.
8. Mytton Papers, Ludlow volume, Birmingham University Library.
9. Hatfield House Papers, parts 11-12 (Hist. Mon. Comm., 1906-10), p. 311.
10. *D.N.B.*
11. Halliwell, J. O., *Notice of Players acting at Ludlow selected from original manuscripts belonging to the Corporation of that town* (1867).
12. Harriett, J., *Shakespeare's Son-in-law: John Hall, Man and Physician* (1964); this contains a facsimile of Hall's *Select Observations on English Bodies* (1679), which has the details of the treatment given to the Countess of Northampton on p. 84.
13. *D.N.B.*
14. Morris, C., *The Illustrated Journeys of Celia Fiennes, 1685-c.1712* (1675), p. 185.
15. W. P. R., *A Short Address to the Inhabitants of Ludlow respecting the Improvement of that Town* (1810; only known copy in Shropshire Local Studies Library).
16. 'Curious Account of Ludlow by a Tourist of 1772', *Salopian Shreds and Patches*, Vol. 1, (1874-75), pp. 104/5.
17. p. 135.
18. George Lipscomb, *Journey into South Wales in the year 1799* (1802), pp. 234-5.
19. Henry James, *Portraits of Places* (1877), Macmillan's edn., 1883, p. 270.
20. pp. 184-88.
21. pp. 168-9.

# Ludlow

# DOMESDAY BOOK, 1086, AND THE EARLY DEVELOPMENT OF LUDLOW

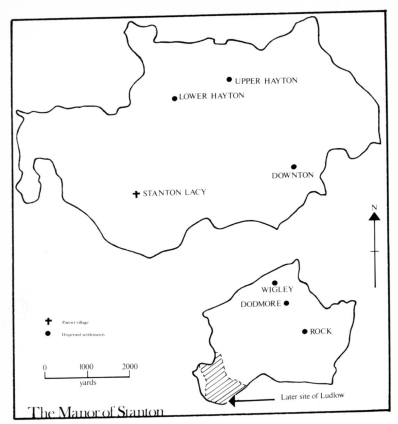

The Manor of Stanton

Parent village

Dispersed settlements

Later site of Ludlow

It is now accepted that the site of medieval Ludlow was once part of the manor of Stanton Lacy. The Domesday survey of 1086 gives a detailed account of *Stantone*, then held by Roger Lacy (d. c.1106), who had succeeded to vast estates when his father Walter died the previous year.[1] The interpretation of the Domesday Book is a skilled and sophisticated process but it can be shown that *Stantone*, which had land for 50 ploughs, was one of the largest and richest manors in Shropshire.[2]

### A translation of the Domesday account of Stantone (Stanton Lacy)[3]

*The same Roger holds Stantone. Siward held it and was a free man. There 20½ hides pay geld. There is land for 50 ploughs. In demesne there are 10 ploughs and 28 serfs and bondwomen together and 67 villeins and 2 smiths and 5 bordars and 4 'cozets'. Among them all they have 23 ploughs. A church is there which has 1½ hides, and 2 priests with 2 villeins have 3 ploughs. 2 mills there of 26 shillings. St Peter of Hereford has there 1 villein. Of the land of this manor Richard holds 1½ hides, Azelin 1½ hides, Roger 1½ hides. These men have in demesne 6 ploughs and 6 serfs, and 2 'semi-villeins', and 5 bordars and 2 'cozets', with 1 plough and a mill of 10 shillings. Out of the same manor 4 serjeants have land for 3 ploughs and 1 ferling and 10 acres of land and they have 4 ploughs. 3 'radchenisters' are there holding land for 2½ ploughs, and have there that number of ploughs. And one man, Auti, holds one member of this manor, in which are 3 hides, and has there 1 plough with a 'semi-villein'. T.R.E. the whole manor was worth 24 pounds. Now 25 pounds.*

**Glossary.** *Demesne:* land retained by the manorial lord on which tenants gave free service; *Geld:* tax based on land; *Hide:* the amount of land which could be ploughed in a year with one plough, usually between 60 and 120 acres depending on the soil; *Radchenister:* a tenant who gave service on horseback for his land; *Serjeant:* a tenant who gave personal service for his land, e.g. tailor or gamekeeper; *T.R.E.:* time of King Edward (the Confessor), i.e. before 1066.

*This little sketch of Stanton Lacy church, made in 1846, shows the strip pilasters and other Saxon features.[4]*

The Domesday survey is arguably the earliest document which encompasses Ludlow, yet it yields no information whatsoever on the site of the town. Stanton Lacy has the dispersed settlement characteristic of the Welsh borders, and it is perhaps significant that the earliest place names—Stanton itself, Lower and Upper Heyton, Wootton and Downton—are all in the north, whereas place names in the south—Wigley, Dodmore, Rock—suggest later colonisation of land which was wooded or waste. This indicates 6th or 7th century settlement in the north, as the first wave of Anglo-Saxons moved along Corve Dale, and then later development towards the south.

Architectural evidence supports the later assertions that Roger de Lacy started to build a castle on a natural defensive site at the southern end of Stanton Lacy parish. It is argued that this was after the Domesday survey of 1086 but before the banishment of Roger for rebellion in 1094.[5] The Castle was part of a line of defences along the Marches erected by the Normans to hold back the still unconquered Welsh. Although there is no evidence of earlier settlement here, at least two

1. Wightman, pp.166-70.
2. Darby, H.C. and Terrett, I.B., *The Domesday Geography of Midland England* (1954), p.133.
3. *V.C.H.* vol. 1 (1908), p.347.
4. Petit, J.L., 'Stanton Lacy Church . . .', *Archaeological Journal*, 1846, p.297.
5. St John Hope (1908), p.324.

ancient roads intersected in the vicinity while there was a bronze age tumulus on part of the site later occupied by the Parish Church.[6] These ancient roads, and perhaps others converging from the east, did much to determine the plan of Ludlow when it was laid out as a new town in the 12th century.[7]

There is no firm evidence of exactly when Ludlow was laid out as a planned town, but it probably occurred in phases. Such towns brought profits to seigneurial lords and by serving as market centres helped to pacify the surrounding countryside. A civilian settlement called 'Lodelowe' was probably in existence before 1138, though there may have been an earlier hamlet at Dinham, just south of the Castle. Analysis of the town plan shows burgage plots of various sizes but nearly all have widths which are multiples of 16½ ft., the standard medieval measurement known as the pole or perch. There were burgages at the bottom of Corve Street before 1186 and this and other evidence shows that the projected town plan was an ambitious one, covering a much larger area than that which was walled in the 13th century.[8] Locative surnames indicate that settlers came in from the surrounding rural manors and from further afield, and that the planned town was successful, so much so that in 1199 the first Parish Church had to be completely rebuilt.

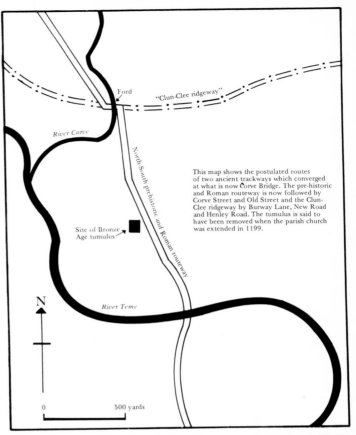

This map shows the postulated routes of two ancient trackways which converged at what is now Corve Bridge. The pre-historic and Roman routeway is now followed by Corve Street and Old Street and the Clun-Clee ridgeway by Burway Lane, New Road and Henley Road. The tumulus is said to have been removed when the parish church was extended in 1199.

0       500 yards

(Above) A view eastwards from the Castle along the line of the 12th-century High Street, the original market place. The High Street can be traced to the top of the picture. The market place was colonised by later buildings, especially the three parallel 'rows' in the middle distance now separated by Church Street, Harp Lane, High Street and Market Street.

(Left) A view from the parish church tower looking north-north-east towards Stanton Lacy. The almost straight line of Corve Street follows a north-south Roman and pre-historic routeway. East-west burgages can also be seen, those on the east running back to Portcullis Lane, the old parish boundary.

6. Cranage, pp. 105-6; Chitty, L., 'The Clun-Clee Ridgeway: a prehistoric track across south Shropshire' in Foster, I., and Alcock, I., Culture and Environment (1963); Houghton, A. W. J., 'A Roman Road from Ashton, North Herefordshire, to Marshbrook, Salop', T.S.A.S., vol. lviii (1964).
7. Conzen, pp. 122-27.
8. Work in preparation for publication by L.H.R.G.

*This detail of a 13th-century manuscript from St Albans Abbey shows how the medieval chronicles were written.*[1]

Most of the writers and historians of the Middle Ages belonged to the church, which had a near monopoly of learning. Using earlier documents and oral reports they produced long histories or chronicles which often began at the Incarnation and continued to the time of writing. They were written on parchment folios, usually beautifully decorated, but later copies have survived more often than the originals. Some of the histories were printed in the 16th and 17th centuries but today they are most readily available in the Rolls series, published from 1858 onwards.

Each chronicler wrote his own mixture of national and local events but no less than eight refer to Ludlow Castle in 1138 and 1139, when civil war had broken out between Stephen and Matilda.[2] These references show that the place name 'Lodelowe' (meaning 'hill by the loud waters') was in use by 1138 but whether it referred to the Castle only or to the Castle and town together is not certain.

The earliest and most reliable chronicler was Henry of Huntingdon (c.1084-1155), an east-country priest who became Archdeacon of Huntingdon and was asked by his bishop to write a history of England.[3] The first edition, written in 1129, was based on Bede and other early chroniclers but later editions, issued up to 1154, cover contemporary events.[4] These include the civil war at the beginning of Stephen's reign, when Ludlow Castle was held against the king by Gervase Pagnal, one of several rebel barons who supported Matilda's claim to the throne.

Describing the events of 1138 the chronicler reports that: *Paganellus (tenuit) castellum de Ludelowe*, i.e. that Pagnal held the Castle of Ludlow. More detail is given for 1139 when Stephen, supported by the young Prince of Scotland, attacked Ludlow. Henry of Huntingdon describes how the prince was nearly caught by a grappling iron and was saved only by the personal intervention of the king. The story was afterwards used to illustrate Stephen's bravery and helped to create an image of *bellator robustimus*, i.e. doughtiest fighter.[5]

1. Bodley MS. 602, f.36.
2. R.S. 36, 43, 51, 57, 75, 82.
3. *D.N.B.*
4. R.S. 75: T.Arnold (Ed.), *Henrici Archidiacon Huntendunensis Historia Anglorum* (1879), pp.261, 265.
5. Barlow,F., *The Feudal Kings of England 1042-1216* (1972), p.89.

*Henricum igitur filium regis Scotorum secum ducens in Angliam, obsedit Ludelowe, ubi idem Henricus unco ferreo equo abstractus paene captus est, sed ipse rex eum ab hostibus splendide retraxit . . .*

'Having led Henry the son of the king of Scotland into England, (Stephen) attacked Ludlow when the same Henry having been almost dragged from his horse by a grappling iron would have been captured had not the king himself bravely rescued him from his enemies.'

The story is repeated almost word for word by two other 12th century chroniclers: Roger of Howden (d.1189), a clerk of Henry II; and Robert of Torigni (c.1110-86), who was Abbot of Mont St Michael off the coast of Normandy, a place visited by many English travellers, including Henry of Huntingdon himself.[6] Thirteenth-century monastic chroniclers copied the story again, e.g. Matthew Paris (c.1200-59) of the important abbey at St Albans.[7]

A much later chronicle is that of Melsa, an abbey in east Yorkshire, which was compiled in the late 14th century by Abbot Burton, using 'ancient documents and parchments'.[8] The events at Ludlow in 1138 and 1139 are included in Chapter 21, which contains abstracts of the affairs of state from the death of Henry I in 1135. These abstracts have been copied from earlier documents but though there is no clear cause to doubt their authenticity they are less reliable than contemporary accounts. Ludlow is one of seven places mentioned but the reference is to the towns as well as to the castles, implying that the new town of 'Lodelowe' was already in existence.

*Quo quidem tempore castra et villas de Herforth, Brystowe, Slede, Kary, Ludelaw, Oxenforth et Maltona, necnon et alia plurima, magnates quidam, regi invidentes et imperatrici confaventes, invasa contra regem Stephanum detinebant. Quae tamen omnia idem rex Stephanum postea regressus recuperavit.[9]*

'At which time certain magnates, opponents of the king and favourites of the empress, making war against King Stephen, occupied the castles and *towns* of Hereford, Bristol, Slede, Kerry, Ludlow, Oxford and Malton, as well as others besides, all of which however the same King Stephen afterwards recovered again.'

*The exact place where King Stephen rescued Prince Henry cannot be identified but the four-storey tower shown on the photograph was certainly standing by 1139, having been raised a few years earlier from the original gatehouse. The tower on the left was at one of the corners of the original Castle and is an early example of a flanking tower.*

6. R.S. 51: *Chronica Magistri Rogeri de Houedene* (1868), 1, pp.193, 196; R.S. *Chronicle of Robert of Torigni* (1889), pp.134, 136.
7. R.S. 57: *The Greater Chronicle of Matthew Paris* (1875), 2, pp.167, 170.
8. R.S. 43: *Chronica Monasterii de Melsa* (1851), p.17.
9. Ibid, p.120.

This is a prose tale in Anglo-Norman French, written in the early 14th century but based on a late 13th century verse romance which is now lost. It traces the fortunes of the Fitzwarine family of Whittington in north Shropshire from the Norman Conquest to the early 13th century.

The romance has been described as 'a weird mixture of accurate information, plausible stories that lack confirmation, and magnificent flights of pure imagination'.[1] A recent authoritative study shows that 'the poet author of the romance belonged to Ludlow in the early Edwardian period' and is at his best when 'on home ground writing about Ludlow castle'.[2] The Ludlow references all occur early in the romance when the hero is the first Fouke Fitzwarine. He is shown as a young squire of Joce de Dinan, lord of Ludlow. Modern research has confirmed that Joce did exist and was active on the Welsh border in the 1140s and early 1150s, a confused period of civil war. He may well have held Ludlow during this period and the romance portrays him as in conflict with its rightful heirs, the Lacys.[3]

An early passage is important for the study of Ludlow's origins and early growth, for it suggests that the first civilian settlement was in the part of the town now called Dinham:

Original Anglo-French version:

*Le chastel de Dynan e tut le pays entours devers la ryvere de Corve ou tut l'onour dona a monsire Joce, sun chevaler, e d'en apres retint le surnoun de Dynan e fust apele par tut Joce de Dynan. Cely Joce parfist le chastiel . . . e si fust fort e vaylaunt chevaler. E si fust la ville bien longement apelle Dynan, qe or est apellee Ludelawe. Cesti Joce fist fere desouth la ville de Dynan un pount de pere e chaus outre la ryvere de Temede, en le haut chemyn qe va parmy la marche, e de Cestre desque Brustul. Joce fist son chastiel de Dynan de tres baylees e le envyrona de double fosse, une dedens e une dehors.*

English translation:

*The Castle of Dynan and all the land thereabout towards the river of Corve, with all the honour, he gave to Sir Joce, his knight; who thenceforth took the name of Dynan and was always called Joce de Dinan. This Joce finished the castle . . . he was a brave knight. And the town which is now called Ludelowe was for a very long time called Dynan. Under the town of Dynan this Joce caused to be built a bridge of stone and lime over the river of Temede, in the high road which runs through the March and from Chester to Bristol. Joce made his Castle with three baillies and encircled it with a double ditch the one within and the other without.*

The next section of the romance is the most eventful. Though there are some inaccuracies a succinct summary was published by the antiquarian Dugdale in 1663 and was repeated some 50 years later by Edward Lloyd of Drenewydd, one of Shropshire's first historians:[4]

*King Henry the First gave Dinan or Ludlow, with the territory of Corvedale, to a Norman knight known by the name of de Dinan; between whom and Walter de Lacy, Lord of Ewias by right of conquest, there arose several contests, whether out of emulation or about fixing the boundaries of their royalties is not known. In one of these skirmishes the said Sir Walter de Lacy and his trusty knight, Sir Ernauld de Lis, were taken prisoners of war, and carried to Dinan, where being in custody, by intriguing with a fair damsel, Mariana de Bruer, they found a way to make their escape. The story goes, that Sir Ernauld coming to the Castle in the absence of . . . the owner, and making his addresses to the lady that procured his enlargement, to be admitted, which she complying with, he seized the Castle upon his entry in a hostile manner; and that afterwards Mariana, to revenge the treachery of her gallant, murdered him in his bed: that (Joce) was obliged, in order to recover his own Castle, to lay siege to it; and that Lacy, with the assistance of the Welsh, beat his force off, and took him prisoner. The sequel contains some inconsistencies, which indeed make the whole narrative fabulous . . .*

1. Palmer,S., *The Reign of King John* (1949), p. 127.
2. Hathaway,E.J., Ricketts,P.T., Robson,C.A., and Wiltshire,A.D., *Fouke Fitz Waryn* (Anglo-Norman texts, 1975), p.36
3. Wightman,W.E., *The Lacy Family in England and Normandy, 1066-1194* (1966), pp.180-1, 187-8. For further confirmation of many details of this conflict see 'The Anglo-Norman Chronicle of Wigmore Abbey', *T.W.N.F.C.*, 39 (1969), p.429
4. Jukes, p.60

*Ludford Bridge, seen on a Frith postcard of the early 20th century. The bridge was rebuilt in the 15th century but probably contains remnants of the 12th century bridge built by Joce de Dinan. Oliver Baker, in 1888, argued that this was a Norman structure, citing 'the enormous bulk of its weedy and rugged piers, together with the character of its square and solid masonry . . .'[5]*

The story was popularised by Thomas Wright who paraphrased the original text in his *History of Ludlow* (1852). A climax occurs when Marian discovers her lover's treachery:

*At daybreak Marian, who was in bed with her lover Sir Arnold, was awakened by the shouts of the victors; she arose, and, looking through a window, learnt the treason which had been acted during the night. In the agony of despair, she seized upon Sir Arnold's sword and thrust it through his body, and immediately afterwards threw herself out of a window which looked towards Linney and broke her neck.[6]*

This part of the romance has been much featured in local guidebooks, e.g. George Woolley, the Bull Ring bookseller, gave it eight of 50 pages on the Castle in the 1905 edition of his *Ludlow Guide*. The story has also caught the imagination of travellers and topographical writers, e.g. in 1939 S.P.B. Mais concluded his chapter on Ludlow in *Highways and By-ways of the Welsh Marches* by observing:

*So there was plenty for me to think about as I clambered up and down these stone staircases . . . but the story that kept on recurring most vividly to my mind was that of the ill-starred Maid Marion . . .[7]*

Good stories grow in the telling so it is perhaps not too surprising to find a writer in a contemporary American magazine both identifying the location of the tragedy and repeating the local tradition of a ghost:

*Marion stabbed her lover . . . and then leaped to her death from . . . Pendover Tower . . . to this day the ghostly figure of a young girl is said to be seen haunting the ruins on moonless nights . . .[8]*

5. Baker,O., *Ludlow; Town and Neighbourhood* (1888), pp. 75-76.
6. p.58
7. p.120
8. Kuhn,I.C., 'Ludlow—a Shropshire Sojourn', *Gourmet*, November 1980, p.26

Giraldus de Barri, commonly called Cambrensis (c.1146-c.1220), was a native of Pembrokeshire who became a court official, a churchman and a writer. In 1188 he accompanied the Archbishop of Canterbury on a journey through Wales and its borders to recruit supporters for Richard I's expedition to the Holy Land later known as the third Crusade. He wrote an account of this journey called *Itinerarium Cambriae*, though this was not printed until 1585.[1]

The journey began at Hereford and went round Wales in a clockwise direction, so that Ludlow was one of the last places visited. There is no evidence that the party stopped at Ludlow but the phrase 'the noble castle' suggests that they noted its fine position, seen to best advantage from the road between Bromfield and Ludlow (now Burway Lane). It is not clear from documentary or architectural evidence whether the outer bailey had yet been built but even without this extension the original late 11th century Castle would have been an imposing sight.

A transcription of the Latin text is given below, followed by a translation published in 1806:

*Transivimus autem a Wenlock per cellulam de Brumfeld, per nobile castrum de Ludlow, per Leonis manasterium usque Herefordiam, Melenyth et Elvel a dextra relictis; a puncto quo per Walliam laboriosum hoc iter arripuimus, tanquam in circino circumeundo, ad punctum denuo jam reversi.*

*In hujus itaque legationis longo laudabilique labore, circiter tria virorum millia crucis signaculo sunt insignita, lanceis et sagittis expeditissima martiisque negotiis exercitatissima . . .*[2]

Translation:

*From Wenlock, we passed by the little cell of Brumfeld,*[3] *the noble castle of Ludlow, through Leominster to Hereford, leaving on our right hand the districts of Melenyth and Elvel; thus (describing as it were a circle) we came to the same point from which we had commenced this laborious journey through Wales.*

*During this long and laudable legation, about three thousand men were signed with the cross; well skilled in the use of arrows and lances, and versed in military matters . . .*[4]

Though this extract has little information on Ludlow it is of great interest as the earliest known description of any part of the town.

*A view of Ludlow from the north west, taken from a field adjoining Burway Lane. This is essentially the view seen by Giraldus in 1188 though the details on the skyline would have been different. If the town's first church had a tower it would have been more squat than its 15th century successor while the imposing range of domestic buildings at the Castle were not built for another century. Ridge and furrow can be seen in the foreground but these meadows bordering the River Teme are now used for pasture.*

1. *D.N.B.*; introduction in Hoare,R.C. (Ed.), *The Itinerary of Archbishop Baldwin through Wales by Giraldus de Barri* (1806).
2. *Itinerarium Cambriae* (1806), p.159.
3. Bromfield Priory two miles north west of Ludlow, which became a cell of St Peter's Abbey, Gloucester, in 1155 (*V.C.H.*, 2, p.27). Bartlett,S.E., writing on the Priory, says that 'the procession which passed along the road to Ludlow' would have been 'led by the banner of S. Thomas of Canterbury, the Archbishop following, with his crosier in his hands, but clad in armour, as prepared for personal combat with the Infidel . . . and an array following him of knights and esquires' (*Records of Gloucester Cathedral*, vol.2, 1883-4, p.56).
4. Hoare,R.C., op. cit., p.186.

Two of these, compilers of the chronicles of Dunstable and Worcester, give important information about Laurence de Lodelowe (d.1294), the best known of Ludlow's medieval wool and cloth merchants. Much of the town's prosperity was based on these commodities. One of the most active Ludlow merchants in the mid-13th century was Nicholas, son of Andrew Fitz Milo.[1] Nicholas also operated in Shrewsbury, where he was known as Nicholas de Lodelowe. Nicholas died in 1278 but his business was extended by his sons, especially by Laurence de Lodelowe. It is clear from the chroniclers' accounts that Laurence was a figure of national standing and one of the richest men of his day:

## ANNALES DE DUNSTAPLIA, 1294

*Laurentius de Lodelowe, nominatissimus mercatorum, submersus est in mari . . . Eodem anno quidam Anglici mercatores de licentia regis cum lanis suis transfretaverunt, quibis praeesse debuit Laurentius de Lodelowe et clericus domini regis supradicti, salvo conducto piratorum lanas quas vendiderunt.*

Translation:
Laurence of Ludlow, the most renowned of merchants, was drowned at sea . . . In the same year certain English merchants, licensed by the King, crossed the sea with their wool; these ought to have been led by Laurence of Ludlow and the clerk of the lord King aforesaid (and) they sold the wool with the safe-conduct of the pirates.[2]

## ANNALES DE WIGORNIA, 1294

*Decimo quarto Kal., ejusdem mutuo cepimus de Laurentio de Lodelowe Londoniis c. mercas quas obligamur eidem xiv. Kal. Junii sequenti anno proximo salvere . . . Laurentius, mercator nominatissimus, periit in mari et corpus ejus delatum fuit apud Lodelowe, et ibi vicesimo Decembris die traditum fuerat sepulturae . . .*

Translation:
14 Kal. of the same we have mutually borrowed from Laurence of Ludlow and of London 100 marks which we are bound to repay to him on 14 Kal. of June following in the next year . . . Laurence, the most renowned of merchants, perished at sea and his body was carried to Ludlow and there on 20 December he was taken to burial . . .[3]

The narrow frontage shop in Drapers' Row now No. 13 King Street (Home Decorators) was one of four messuages and seven shops held by Sir Laurence de Lodelowe (d.1353), grandson of the great clothier. Some of these properties were bought by Laurence between 1286 and 1288.[4]

The hall of Stokesay Castle, built by Laurence de Lodelowe c.1280. The tall, two-light windows are a prominent feature. It is a measure of Laurence's influence that in 1291 he had licence to defend Stokesay by the crenallated southern tower on the left of the photograph. This is taken from one of many Frith postcards published of Stokesay in the early 20th century.

1. Eyton, pp.36.
2. *Annales Monasticii* (R.S. no.58, 1866), vol.3, 'Annals of Dunstable', pp.389-90.
3. Ibid, vol.4, 'Annals of Worcester', pp.510, 518.
4. PRO: Feet of Fines, CP 25 (1), 193-6, nos.25,26.

RAPHAEL HOLINSHED
AND
CHRISTOPHER MARLOWE
DESCRIBING EVENTS
OF THE
EARLY 14th CENTURY

Raphael Holinshed (d.1580) was a native of Cheshire who came to London to work as a translator. He edited the *Chronicles* which contain the works of both earlier and contemporary authors though commonly known under his name. The chapter on Edward II, king between 1307 and 1327, provided the plot and much of the detail for a play of that name by Christopher Marlowe (1564-93).

The context of the play is the power struggle between the weak king and his favourites on the one hand and powerful discontented barons on the other. The barons were led by Roger Mortimer of Wigmore and Ludlow, who is included in Marlowe's full title:

*The troublesome raigne and lamentable death of Edward the second, king of England, with the tragicull fall of proud Mortimer.*

Roger Mortimer (1287-1330) is remembered as the most ambitious of the remarkable Mortimer family who had held Wigmore Castle since the Norman Conquest. In 1306 he married Joan Geneville, heiress of a moiety of Ludlow, and Ludlow Castle became an important power base for his political activities.[1] He was involved in the Scottish wars and in successful moves against the king's favourites but in 1323 he was imprisoned in the Tower of London. Holinshed tells the story of his escape:

*About the same time the lord Roger Mortimer of Wigmor, giving his keepers a drinke that brought them into a sound and heavie sleepe, escaped out of the tower of London where he was prisoner. This escape of the lord Mortimer greatlie troubled the king, so that immediately upon the first news he wrote to all the shiriffs of the realm, that if he chanced to come within their rooms they should cause hue and crie to be raised, so as he might be staied and arrested, but he made such shift, that he got over into France . . .*

*A fine range of domestic buildings on the north side of the inner bailey, built in the late 13th and early 14th centuries, when Ludlow Castle was transformed from a military bastion into a fortified palace. The Great Hall, in the centre of the picture, and the service block on the left were built before Roger Mortimer acquired the Castle, probably by Peter de Geneville, his father-in-law. The residential range on the right, with the Great Chamber on the first floor, was added by Mortimer c. 1320. Queen Isabella and her courtiers were entertained here in 1328.*

1. Moir, pp. 6-9; this is a convenient summary of the considerable information known about Mortimer.

In France Mortimer allied himself with Queen Isabella who had deserted her effeminate husband. They raised an army, invaded England and forced Edward to abdicate in favour of his young son, Edward III. In a memorable scene Marlowe puts in dramatic form the statement by Holinshed that: *the whole government rested in a manner betwixt the queene mother and him . . .*

*Line 2147, Mortimer to Queene Isabell:*

*Be rulde by me, and we will rule the realme; In any case, take heed of childish feare,*
*For now we hould an ould Wolfe by the ears, That if he slip will seize upon us both,*
*And gripe the sorer being gript himselfe. Thinke therefore madam that imports us much*
*To erect your sonne with all the speed we may, And that I be protector over him,*
*For our behalfe will bear the greater sway, When as a king's man shall be underwrit!*

*Queen: Sweet Mortimer, the life of Isabell, Be thou persuaded, that I love thee well,*
*And therefore so the prince my sonne be safe, Whome I esteeme as deare as these mine eyes,*
*Conclude against his father what thou wilt, And I myselfe will willinglie subscribe.*

Edward II was cruelly murdered in Berkeley Castle while Mortimer entertained Isabella at his castles along the Welsh border. At Ludlow there was 'great expense in feasts, tiltings and other recreations'.[2] But before long Mortimer over-reached himself, arousing the envy of rival barons. In October 1330 he was arrested at Nottingham and was sentenced to death and executed at Tyburn. Marlowe gives him an impressive farewell speech:

*Line 2627: Base fortune, now I see, that in thy wheele,*
*There is a point, to which men aspire,*
*They tumble hedlong downe: that point I touce,*
*And seeing there was no place to mount up higher,*
*Why should I greave at my declining fall?*
*Farewell faire Queene, weepe not for Mortimer,*
*That scorns the world, and as a traveller*
*Goes to discover countries yet unknown.*

*The Garderobe Tower behind the residential block, seen from outside the Castle. The tower contains four floors of bedrooms, some of which had their own garderobes. On the ground and second floors the small windows of the garderobe chambers can be seen, paired with the larger bedroom windows.*

*The ruins of the chapel of St Peter, built in the outer bailey of Ludlow Castle by Roger Mortimer to celebrate his escape from the Tower of London on St Peter's Day, 1323. The chapel was much altered in the 16th century, when it became a courthouse of the Council of the Marches.[3]*

2. A chronicler quoted by Weyman (1911), p. 24.
3. St John Hope (1908); all information about the architectural history of the Castle is from this source.

St Laurence's Parish Church has a remarkable series of 28 misericords which are justly famous and rival those in cathedrals such as Gloucester and Worcester. They are to be found in the choir stalls on either side of the High Chancel, the part of the church reserved for the use of the clergy in the Middle Ages. During Mass the priests, deacons and clerks were obliged to stand but could support themselves by the elbow rests on the side of each stall and by the corbels of the misericords which were carved upon the under surfaces of the hinged seats. Each seat was carved out of a solid piece of timber some 26 in. long, 12 in. deep and 6 in. thick and by tradition was often embellished with vivid medieval imagery.

Although all the misericords are stylistically very similar they appear to have been the result of at least two phases of carving. The eight earliest may date from the late 14th century, with a carver's mark in the form of an uprooted plant. The profile of the moulding running around the edge of the corbel is also distinctive. Most of the remainder seem to have been carved to match in 1447, towards the end of the rebuilding of the chancel in the fashionable Perpendicular style of the day. In that year the Palmers' Guild acquired 100 planks of oak from Bristol 'to make new stalls'. The Guild, founded in the mid-13th century, did much to beautify the Church and to provide music for its services. The subjects of the misericords are very varied but several of them provide rare glimpses of the domestic and commercial life of medieval Ludlow.

*The seated figure on the left is damaged but may be a wet-nurse or a schoolmaster. In the centre a prosperous citizen is surrounded by the tools and products of various trades. On the right is a grave with burial implements. The whole design may represent the Palmers' Guild, who cared for its members throughout life and prayed for their souls after death; if so, the central figure is the Warden.*

*This figure is often described as a pedlar with his bundle, but he could equally well be a merchant's porter, drawing on his boots to take a wool-pack to market. In 1472 480 cloths were sealed by the Ludlow alnager, each cloth containing 100 pieces. Heavy cloths called 'Ludlow Whytes' were well known and fetched good prices in London.*

A figure in late 14th century costume drawing ale or wine from a barrel. He is sometimes interpreted as a fuddled drinker with his head resting on his hands, and often nicknamed 'Simon the cellarer'. Leases and other documents show that many taverns of 15th century Ludlow were in cellars, e.g. what is now No. 1 Old Street had a barrel vault and was used as an air-raid shelter during World War Two but was filled up in 1963.

Another tavern scene showing the terrible fate of a dishonest Ludlow ale-wife. On the left a demon reads out her misdeeds from a long scroll. A second demon, decapitated by later vandals, has the miscreant over his shoulder, though she stubbornly clutches on to her short measure. A third demon plays the bagpipes as an accompaniment to her journey while a fourth waits to receive her at the gaping maw of hell.

The central hooded figure warms himself by the hearth while a kettle bubbles on another fire and two flitches hang from the ceiling. There is no sign of a chimney and this is probably an open hearth in the middle of a hall, like those identified at Nos. 40 and 53 Broad Street. The carving is perhaps a homily on wisely laying in stores for a bleak winter or it may be just a symbol for winter. A similar misericord is to be found at Worcester Cathedral.

This misericord is much damaged but evidently shows a wrestling match, a popular sport in the 15th century. The two pairs of wrestlers are stripped to the waist. On the left is a bystander. On the right are a woolsack and a purse, presumably the prizes for the winner. The horse may also be part of a wager.

The stained glass of Ludlow Parish Church is 'full of interest' in spite of 'the considerable amount of restoration and remaking'.[1] Much of it dates from the middle years of the 15th century, when the central part of the Parish Church was rebuilt, using the fashionable Perpendicular style of the day. So much glass was needed at this time that there 'might have been a workshop in the town', but no evidence of this has so far been revealed. The windows are primarily artistic works but in spite of the stylized designs they are also an important historical record giving details of contemporary costumes, furniture and utensils.

The three panels reproduced on these pages are all from the Annunciation or Golden Window, which is generally regarded as the finest in the church. The window is on the north wall of the chapel of St John the Evangelist, which was the special chapel of the Palmers' Guild (see pp.26-27). Like others in the church, the window had a teaching function and lines of the Pater Noster are written between the panels.

This panel is part of the Annunciation scene and shows the Virgin Mary, with her arms crossed in humility. From the upper left hand corner divine rays descend from the Father in Heaven. Rich blues and reds are used to portray the costume of an upper-class lady of the mid-15th century. The jewels on the embroidered band round the red cloak are a distinctive Ludlow feature.

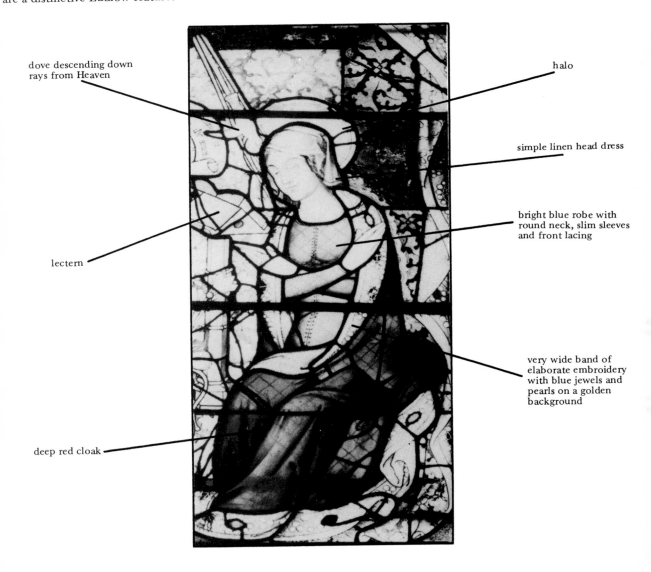

dove descending down rays from Heaven

halo

simple linen head dress

bright blue robe with round neck, slim sleeves and front lacing

lectern

very wide band of elaborate embroidery with blue jewels and pearls on a golden background

deep red cloak

1. Ganderton,E.W. and Lafond,J., *Ludlow Stained and Painted Glass* (1961), p.52. All quotations in this paragraph are from this source.

The two panels on this page are at the bottom of the window and show the donors and their children. A remnant of an inscription reads: *Katerina uxoris ei (us hanc fenestram) fieri fecerunt*—'Katherine his wife caused (this window) to be made'.

The donors may have been John Parys and his wife Katherine. John Parys made his will in November 1449 and directed that his body 'be buried in the parish church of St. Laurence in the chancel of St. John'.[2] He was one of the leading Ludlovians of his day, being Bailiff in 1429-30, 1439-40 and 1443-44, and serving as Warden of the Palmers' Guild from 1442 until his death.[3] His father, William Parys, is often described as a draper and John himself is known to have sold wool, for in 1422 he and others were charged at the King's Bench for selling sacks of wool 'against the Statute'.[4] The Parys family lived at the important building known as 'the house with the leaden porch', now Nos.16 - 18 Castle Street.

All four figures are portrayed in white, gold and black only; but the low walled enclosures which enclose them are in a beautiful golden ochre colour. There are stylized plants around the walls and the floor is tiled in black and white chequer board fashion. Both adults and children are kneeling at prayer stools.

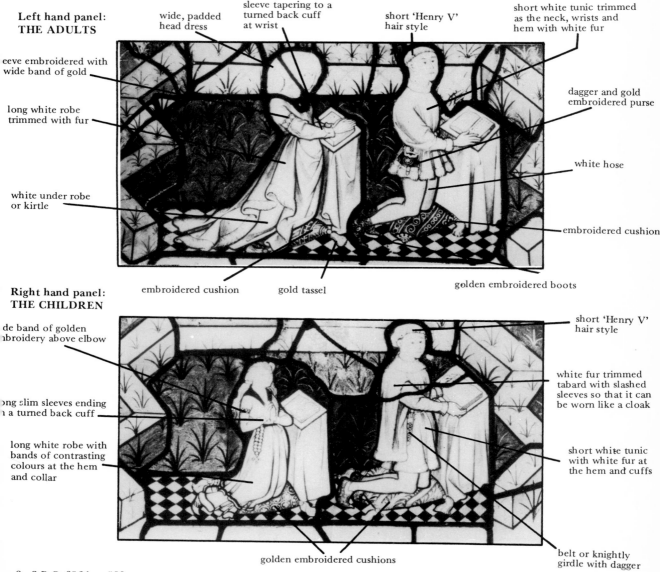

**Left hand panel: THE ADULTS**

- wide, padded head dress
- sleeve tapering to a turned back cuff at wrist
- short 'Henry V' hair style
- short white tunic trimmed as the neck, wrists and hem with white fur
- sleeve embroidered with wide band of gold
- long white robe trimmed with fur
- dagger and gold embroidered purse
- white hose
- white under robe or kirtle
- embroidered cushion
- embroidered cushion
- gold tassel
- golden embroidered boots

**Right hand panel: THE CHILDREN**

- wide band of golden embroidery above elbow
- short 'Henry V' hair style
- white fur trimmed tabard with slashed sleeves so that it can be worn like a cloak
- long slim sleeves ending in a turned back cuff
- long white robe with bands of contrasting colours at the hem and collar
- short white tunic with white fur at the hem and cuffs
- golden embroidered cushions
- belt or knightly girdle with dagger

2. S.R.O. 356 box 520.
3. Ibid, M.T.s 417, 419, 426, 428, 602, 603, 803, 865, 1380.
4. P.R.O., K.B. 23/614, m.37d.

This is the east window of the chapel of St John the Evangelist, which was the special chapel of the Palmers' Guild. The Guild was founded c.1250 as a purely local organisation but after 1390 there was a big expansion in its activities and by the early 16th century it had a nationwide membership of over 4,000 and owned much property, including some 200 tenements, shops and land in Ludlow.[1] Members subscribed fees and made donations, in return for which priests employed by the Guild said prayers and masses in the Parish Church on their behalf, both before and after death.

The window shows a local version of the legend of King Edward the Confessor and St John the Evangelist. Most of the glass is mid-15th century but some of it had been displaced and had to be assembled from different parts of the church when the window was restored in 1878.[2] Historically, there is no connection between King Edward (c.1004-66) and the Palmers' Guild; but when the Guild was founded in the mid-13th century there was a widespread Edward the Confessor cult which was eagerly promoted by King Henry III. This may have encouraged the Guild to adopt the legend.

The story in the window appears in many places, the earliest reference being in the life of Edward written by

Ailred, Abbot of Rievaulx, just a few years after Edward had been canonised in 1161. A modern scholar has written:

> *Among the new miracles there appears for the first time . . . the story of the ring and the pilgrims which was to become the most popular of the legends connected with the saint and gave him the emblem—the ring—with which he is generally represented in medieval art.*[3]

In Westminster Abbey, which was largely rebuilt by Henry III in glorification of Edward, the story is represented five times, the best known being the stone screen in Edward the Confessor's chapel. The screen was completed in 1441, just a few years before the window at Ludlow was made. A frieze at the top of the screen depicts scenes from the King's life, three of which are from the legend. The *Westminster Abbey Official Guide* (1971) reports the tradition that 'the pilgrims are said to have come from Ludlow'.[4]

Panel 2 (left). *King Edward gives the ring to St John who is disguised as a beggar;* Panel 3 (below left). *St John gives the ring to the Ludlow Palmers;* Panel 4 (below right). *King Edward gives the Ludlow Palmers the Guild charter.*

1. Gaydon,A.T., 'Ludlow, Palmers' Guild', *V.C.H.* vol.2 (1973), pp.134-40.
2. Ganderton and Lafond, pp.47-51; Weyman (1925), pp.8-11.
3. Tanner,E.L., 'Some Representations of St Edward the Confessor in Westminster Abbey and elsewhere', *Journal of the British Archaeological Association*, 3rd. ser., vol.15 (1952), p.4.
4. p.100.

The Palmers' window. The upper tracery contains the arms of King Edward the Confessor and the arms of Ludlow. Below are six openings each containing a pennon on which are silver coins.

The upper panels, from left to right:

1. The Ludlow Palmers, wearing their distinctive blue clothes, board a ship for the Holy Land.
2. King Edward the Confessor in a wood. He gives a ring to the beggar who is St John in disguise.
3. St John reveals himself to the Ludlow Palmers and gives them the ring to restore to King Edward. In the legend they are told to inform the King that in six months he will be in Paradise.
4. The Palmers return the ring to the King in England and give him the message.

The lower panels, from left to right:

5. The Palmers in their blue clothes in a religious procession, perhaps to celebrate their safe return.
6. King Edward gives the Ludlow Palmers a document, traditionally identified in this version of the legend as the Guild's charter.
7. The Palmers are greeted on their return to Ludlow by leading citizens, perhaps the Warden of the Guild and members of its ruling Council of Twelve.
8. The Palmers are entertained by the Guild Council, perhaps at one of the grand feasts held in the Guildhall. They are celebrating the acquisition of the Guild's charter.

*(Above) A falcon and fetterlock, from one of the misericords in the Parish Church. Falconry was a popular aristocratic sport. This was the usual emblem of Richard, Duke of York. He had two claims to the throne, one going back to Lionel, Duke of Clarence (1338-68), the second son of Edward III, and the other to Edmund, Duke of York (1341-1402), the fourth son of Edward III.*

*(Below) An antelope with chain and collar, from another misericord. Exotic and foreign beasts were often used for heraldic purposes. This emblem was used by Henry VI (1421-71), the leader of the Lancastrians. His claim to the throne went back to John of Gaunt, Duke of Lancaster (1340-99), the third son of Edward III.*

In the middle years of the 15th century two rival factions struggled for political power. Each faction had a leader with some claim to the throne, the senior line of descent from Edward III having become extinct at the death of Richard II in 1399. Until 1461 the Lancastrians governed the country but in the 1440s and 1450s, when Henry VI was a weak and largely ineffective king, their rule was challenged by the Yorkists. The Yorkist leader was Richard Plantagenet, Duke of York (1411-60), who was also manorial lord of Ludlow through inheritance from his mother, Anne Mortimer. Ludlow Castle was an important Yorkist stronghold but the burgesses of the town seem to have 'hedged their bets', for the roof and choir stalls of the chancel of the Parish Church, rebuilt between 1433 and about 1450, contain both Lancastrian and Yorkist emblems.

As a Yorkist base Ludlow become involved in the sporadic fighting which posterity has called 'the Wars of the Roses'. In October 1459 the Yorkist leaders and their forces had assembled at Ludlow and on 12 October a large Lancastrian army, led by the King himself, advanced from the south and encamped at Ludford, just south of the River Teme.[1] A great battle seemed imminent but during the night a large group of mercenaries, under Andrew Trollope, deserted from the Yorkists and joined the Lancastrians, supposedly because they were unwilling to fight against their king. This created such disparity of numbers that Richard, his son Edward (later King Edward IV) and other Yorkist leaders thought it wise to escape. Next day, 13 October, the Lancastrians had an easy victory at the so-called battle of Ludford and went on to capture Ludlow.

1. A summary of the events of 1459 at Ludlow is given in Clive, M., *This Sun of York: A Biography of Edward IV* (1973), pp.1-7.

*A distant view of Ludford from the tower of Ludlow Parish Church. The cluster of buildings of Ludford village can be seen in the trees, just right of centre. Further left a line of trees marks the incised course of the River Teme. Beyond is the gently sloping ground where the Lancastrian forces encamped on 12 October 1459. There are puzzling earth marks in the area which may be the legacy of hastily constructed defences.*

William Gregory was a master skinner who became Mayor of London in 1451. He wrote the greater part of 'A Chronicle of London', describing national events as seen from the capital up to just before his death in 1466.[1] An unknown writer then took the story to 1469, when the manuscript stops in mid-sentence.

### Gregory's description of the confrontation at Ludlow.

Two passages in Gregory's account of the year 1459-60 relate to Ludlow. The first describes the confrontation and the flight of the Duke of York but omits the defection of Andrew Trollope:

*And thys same yere there was a grete afray at Lodlowe by twyne the kynge and the Duke of Yorke, the Erle of Salusbury, the Erle of Warwyke, the Erle of Marche. The Duke of Yorke lete make a grete depe dyche and fortefyde it with gonnys, cartys, and stakys, but hys party was ovyer weke, for the kyng was mo thenn xxx M. of harneysyd men, by-syde nakyd men that were compellyd for to come with the kynge. And thenne the duke fledde fro place to place in Walys, and breke downe the bryggys aftyr hym that the kyngys mayny schulde not come aftyr hym . . .*

### Gregory's description of the pillaging of Ludlow.

The chronicler describes the fortunes of the refugee Yorkist leaders in Ireland and France and their recruitment of what was eventually a victorious army. Then he returns to describe what happened to Ludlow after they left:

*The mysrewle of the kyngys galentys at Ludlowe, whenn they hadde dronkyn i-nowe of wyne that was in tavernys and in other placys, they full ungoodely smote owte the heddys of the pypys and hoggys hedys of wyne, that men wente wetschode in wyne, and thenn they robbed the towne, and bare a-waye beddynge, clothe, and other stuffe, and defoulyd many wymmen . . .*

Another report on the behaviour of the Lancastrians comes from an entry in the Papal Registers dated 4 May 1465 when the Pope himself promised indulgences for those who gave alms to the Carmelite Friars because: *about 4 years ago as a result of the wars and calamities . . . the House was plundered by men at arms of all its furniture and the friars of all their utensils . . .*[2]

1. Gairdner,J., (Ed.), *The Historical Collections of a Citizen of London in the Fifteenth Century* (Camden Soc., 2nd ser., no.17, 1876), pp.205, 207.
2. *Calendar of Papal Registers, 1458-1471*, p.425.

Richard, Duke of York, was killed in 1460 but early the next year his supporters won a decisive victory at Mortimer's Cross near Ludlow; and on 28 June 1461 Edward IV (1442-83) was crowned at Westminster. By descent from the Mortimers Edward was also manorial lord of Ludlow and for the next 350 years the Castle and the adjoining Castle Meadow (a detached part of Stanton Lacy parish) were Crown property. Almost immediately, however, Edward's manorial rights over the town of Ludlow were transferred to 'the bailiffs, burgesses and commonalty' in a charter which incorporated Ludlow as a Borough. This was dated 7 December 1461.[1] It is clear that many clauses of the charter simply confirmed ancient privileges but there were some new items, e.g. the right of the Borough to send two representatives to Parliament.

The charter begins with a reference to the events of 1459:

*Know ye, that we, considering the laudable and gratuitous services which our beloved and faithful subjects the burgesses of Ludlow have rendered unto us in the obtaining of our right to the crown of England . . . in great peril of their lives: And also the rapines, depredations, oppressions, losses of goods and other grievances for us and our sake . . .*

The charter is the first known document which defines 'the liberties of Ludlow', i.e. the parts of adjoining parishes where Ludlow burgesses enjoyed rights and privileges:

*from the east part of the Borough . . . as far as the township of Rock and from thence as far as the township of Further Halton on the West part . . . and from . . . Further Halton as far as the township of Overton on the South part; and from the same township of Overton as far as the township of Stanton Lacy on the north part; and from thence as far as the . . . township of Rock . . .*

Most of this area was occupied by large open fields. Some of these survived until the late 18th century, e.g. Hucklemarsh Field north of what is now Henley Road and Waretree Field, north of Sheet Road; but others were enclosed at an early date, e.g. there were closes off Halton Lane by the mid-16th century. The south west of the area was occupied by Whitcliffe Common, which was much more extensive than the Common of today.

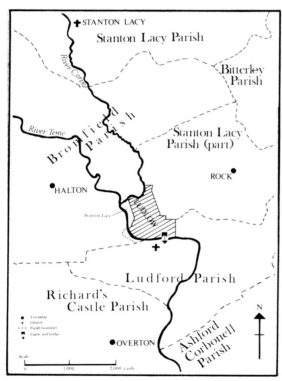

*Map of the Ludlow district, showing the places mentioned in the Charter and the approximate extent of the liberties. There is no evidence that they actually reached as far north as Stanton Lacy.*

*King Edward IV, from the west window of the Parish Church. The glass is the work of T. Williment and was inserted in 1859-60.*

1. Salwey, T.J., *The More Important Municipal Charters of the Borough of Ludlow* (1923), pp.2-20.

Section 24 is one of the most informative in the Charter, for it grants the right to a murage for the defence of the town by means of tolls on goods sold in the market:

*Also we have granted . . . to the aforesaid bailiffs and burgesses . . . that they, by the hands of certain of the good and lawful men . . . whom they shall depute for that purpose . . . for the separation, defendation and fortification of the bridges, ports, towers and walls of the town . . . and for the munition and defence of the same town in the resistance of the rebels of Wales and the Marches thereof, may take, receive, and have yearly for ever, all and singular the customs underwritten:*

| | | | |
|---|---|---|---|
| For every horse load of corn for sale . . . or malt | ¼d. | For every dozen lampreys for sale | 1d. |
| For every tun of wine for sale | 1d. | For every cask of sturgeon for sale | ½d. |
| For every hide of horse and mare, fresh or salt or tanned | ¼d. | For every last of herrings for sale | 6d. |
| For every 5 hogs for sale | ½d. | For every horse load of cinders for sale | ½d. |
| For every 10 porkers | ½d. | For every horse load of honey for sale | 1d. |
| For 10 sheep, goats and pigs for sale | 1d. | For every cart loaded for sale as well | 1d. |
| For every 100 skins of lambs and goats for sale | 1d. | For the week, likewise, for one hundred-weight of pewter | 1d. |
| For every 100 woolfells for sale | 6d. | For every weight of tallow and grease | 1d. |
| For every quarter of salt for sale | ¼d. | For every quarter of gaids sold | 2d. |
| For every horse load of cloth for sale of the value of 40s. | 1d. | For 2,000 of garlick or onions for sale | ½d. |
| For every bale of cloth for sale, brought by cart | 3d. | For every bale of leather for sale | 3d. |
| For every hundred worsted cloths for sale | 2d. | For every 100 of faggots for sale | ¼d. |
| For every cloth or worsted which is called coverlid of value of 40s. | 1d. | For every cart load of timber for sale | ½d. |
| For every 150 webs of aplsham for sale | 1d. | For every hundred of tin, brass or copper for sale | 2d. |
| For every piece of wrought silk for sale | 1d. | For every boat loaded with malt or other things whatsoever, exceeding the value of 20s. | ½d. |
| For every cart load of fish for sale | ½d. | | |
| For every 100 of mullets, salt or dried, for sale | 1d. | For every other merchandize not herein specified of the value of 5s. | 1d. |
| For every horse load of seafish for sale | ¼d. | | |
| For every salmon for sale | ¼d. | | |

This list gives an excellent account of the range of goods available at Ludlow market, held on a Thursday, and at the annual fair, held on the eve, feastday and morrow of St Philip and St James (30 April, 1 and 2 May). Some of the items are illustrated in the stained glass and wood carvings of the period.

*Detail from a misericord, showing a lady's head-dress made from silk and other materials.*

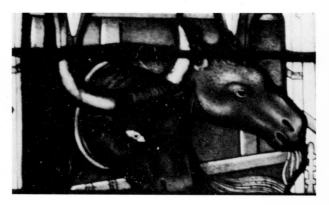

*A cow and a horse, portrayed with St Joseph in one of the Saints windows in the chancel of the Parish Church. The cow, though without the patch introduced by later inter-breeding, is said to be the earliest picture of the Hereford breed.*

A well-known episode in Ludlow's history was the residence there from 1473 to 1483 of Edward and Richard, the sons of King Edward IV. The nobles and gentlemen who attended Prince Edward formed a Council which later became the Council in the Marches of Wales and administered the whole of the principality and its border counties.[1]

Edward (1470-83) and his brother are known to history as 'the little princes in the Tower'. Edward was at Ludlow when his father died on 9 April 1483 and there assumed the title Edward V; but a fortnight later he set out for London, where he and his brother were imprisoned in the Tower and murdered, so that their uncle became King as Richard III.[2] Responsibility for these murders has never been firmly established but Richard had both motive and opportunity. This was certainly the view taken by the Tudors, for after Henry VII had seized the Crown by defeating Richard at Bosworth, it was politic to blacken Richard's name as much as possible.

Sir Thomas More (1478-1535), a lawyer and a humanist scholar, was a loyal Tudor civil servant. His *History of Richard III*, written in 1513, presents Richard as murderer and villain. The passage below confirms other evidence that Prince Edward was in Ludlow when his father died and gives some insight into why he went there, as perceived 30 years later.

> *As soon as the king was departed, the noble prince his sonne drew toward London, which at the time of his decease kept his household at Ludlow in Wales, which countrie being farre off the law and recourse to justice, was begun to be farre out of good rule, and waxed wild robbers and reauvers, walking at libertie uncorrected. And for this occasion the prince was in the life of his father sent thither, to the end that the authoritie of his presence should refrain evil disposed persons from the boldness of their former outrages . . .*[3]

More's work, incorporated in Holinshed's *Chronicles* (see pp. 20-21), was the principal source used by William Shakespeare (1564-1616), who was also eager to please a Tudor monarch. In his play *Richard III*, presented in 1593, Shakespeare follows More closely, both in his portrayal of Richard's character and in historical details, including the presence of Prince Edward at Ludlow when the king dies. The references to Ludlow occur in Act 2, Scene 2, just after the death of Edward IV, when the suggestion to send for Prince Edward comes from the Duke of Buckingham:

> *Though we have spent the harvest of this king,*
> *We are to reap the harvest of his son . . .*
> *Me seemeth good, that, with some little train,*
> *Forthwith from Ludlow the young prince be fet*
> *Hither to London, to be crown'd our king.*

This is agreed and Richard, then Duke of Gloucester, begins to make practical arrangements:

> *Then be it so; and go we to determine*
> *Who they shall be that straight shall post to Ludlow . . .*

1. Williams (1958), pp.7-9
2. Weyman (1911), p.40
3. Maister Thomas Moore, 'The Historie of King Edward the fifth and King Richard the third', 1513, in Holinshed's *Chronicles*, Vol.2 (1577).

# BISHOP ROWLAND LEE, PRESIDENT OF THE COUNCIL IN THE MARCHES OF WALES, 1536

The Council of the Marches had an intermittent existence after 1483 and its powers were limited, even though there was an occasional royal presence at Ludlow Castle: Prince Arthur and his bride Catherine of Aragon for five months in 1501-2 and Princess Mary during the winters of 1525-8. Between 1534 and 1642, however, the Council enjoyed great authority and prestige.[1] Its headquarters were at Ludlow Castle and the town was a specialist administrative centre, fittingly described as a 'bureaucratic anthill'.[2]

It was Rowland Lee (d.1543), appointed Lord President of the Council in 1534, who first established real authority over Wales, and the border counties. The son of a well-bred Northumbrian gentleman, Lee was a successful churchman and civil servant, who owed much to patronage, first of Cardinal Wolsey, then of Thomas Cromwell.[3] He played an important part in the divorce proceedings between Henry VIII and Catherine in 1533 and perhaps received the Bishopric of Lichfield and Coventry as a reward. When he became President of the Council in 1534 he campaigned ruthlessly against the disorder then prevalent in Wales and the letter below is typical of many which he wrote to Cromwell. The references to the market and to the gallows provide added local interest.[4]

*After my most harty recommedacone this shalbe tadvertise you that we have receaved from you the two outlawes named David Lloid or place and John ap Richard hackleton with Richard ap howell als Sumner the murderer of Monmouth for the which we hartely thanke you. And the sayde two outlawes we have sent to their triall according to Justice which to morrow they shall Receyve (god pardon their sowles) and farther within two dayes after the Recyving of the said theves were brought to us iiii other outlawis as greate or greater they the aforesaid david and John were and two of the first of them had been outlawed these xvj yeres, whereof iii now on liffe and oon slayne brought in a sacke trussed uppon the gallowes here for a signe wolde god ye had seen the Fashion thereof but Chanced the same day to be markett daye here, By reason whereof 111C people followed to see the said Cariage of the said thief in the sacke, the manner whereof had not been seen heretofore, what shall we say farther, all the theves in Wales quake for feare, and all this day we do assure you there is but one thief whose name is hugh durant trustying to have him shorteley So that now ye may boldly affirme that Wales is redacte to that state that oone theef taketh an other and oone Cow keepeth another for themoste part as Lewes my servant at his Returne shall mor at large inform you. The takers of thes outlawes were my Lord of Richmonds ten'nts of Keviloke and Arustley most part for feare (and mony) and parte for to have thanks and partly to have some of their kynredd discharged. The names of the sayde Outlawes ensue besechying you that the kyngs highness may be advertised hereof And thus the holy Trinitie preserve you from Ludlowe the xixth. daye of January you(r) Most Bowdon Roland[5]*

*Ludlow Castle: a 19th-century engraving.*

1. Williams, pp.3-46
2. Wanklyn, Dr. M.D.G., *Landed Society and Allegiance in Cheshire and Shropshire in the First Civil War*, Manchester Ph.D., 1967, p.42
3. *D.N.B.*
4. The Ludlow gallows was in Waretree open field on the eastern side of the town, in an area still known as Gallows Bank.
5. *State Papers Henry VIII*, vol.10, no.130

John Leland (c. 1506-52) was a humanist scholar, employed by the government of Henry VIII to search monastic and college libraries for 'monuments of ancient writers'. Between 1538 and 1545 much of his time was spent on 'laborious' journeys round the country collecting topographical and historical information for a projected *Antiquitaties Brittaniae*. Due to failing health this book was never written but nearly all his travel notes survive, either in the original manuscripts or as copies, e.g. that made by John Stowe, another topographical writer, in 1576.[1]

In the 17th century most of the manuscripts and copies were acquired by the Bodleian Library, Oxford, and in 1710-12 they were published as *Leland's Itinerary in England and Wales*, after careful editing by the librarian, Thomas Hearne. Most of the material on Ludlow is in book 5 but the entries are not necessarily in the order in which the journeys were made. Ludlow is one of the few places for which rough notes survive as well as the written-up travel notes. Usually these are jottings which Leland expands and elucidates in his text but where they give additional information they are included below in brackets.

In spite of his knowledge of books it is Leland's power of first-hand observation which has been most valued by later generations. The Ludlow entries reflect his persistent interest in topographical features, bridges and religious foundations. They also illustrate his gift for the memorable phrase, e.g. his description of the Carmelite Friary as 'a fayre and costly thing'. He came to Ludlow in 1540 or later whilst on a circuit of south-east Wales and the border counties.[2] He arrived from the south and left for Bishop's Castle. There is no evidence that he spent a night in the town but he stayed long enough to hear the story of King Edward and the Ludlow pilgrims, to learn something of the lordship of the castle and to take a close look at the church and its tombs. In contrast he says very little about the castle and probably didn't go to that end of the town, for he admits that he 'was not at Mill-gate', while Dinham gate is omitted altogether. It is curious that he didn't mention the Council of the Marches, already well established at the castle. Modern scholarship has confirmed the accuracy of most of his observations, though he did make occasional errors, e.g. the Warden of the Palmers' Guild was elected for life, not annually as Leland reports.

*A stretch of the town wall between Broad Gate and Old Street Gate, bordering what is now St John's Road. This area was landscaped in the 1970s by the South Shropshire District Council and well-cut lawns and flower beds occupy the site of the old town ditch. In Leland's time the ditch was already occupied by limepits and tanpits but it was re-used for military purposes during the 1642-46 Civil War. The wall at the bottom of the garden of No. 2 Brand Lane can be seen on the left. In the corner of the garden, underneath the tree, is a small summer house.*

1. The MSS of Vol. V are in the Bodleian Library, Oxford (Gen.top.e.13). Stowe's MSS, from which the bracketed notes are taken are also in the Bodleian (Tanner, 464, vol. 11, fol. 2). Both are reproduced in L. T. Smith (ed.), Leland's *Itinerary in England and Wales* (1964 ed.), Vol. 11, pp. 76-79.
2. The graves he describes include that of '. . . Sulyard, justicar in the Marchis of Wales', whose will was made on 22 March 1539, and proved on 7 May 1540 (PRO: Prob 11/28 fo. 6). This enables Leland's visit to be dated in 1540 or later.

Transcription of the account of Ludlow.

The bridge upon Tende at Ludlow devidithe withe the streame downe alonge Herfordshire from Shrobbesshire.
The towne of Ludlow being in Shrobbesshire on the left ripe of Teme ryver is set upon an hill; so that a man cumming to it any waye conscendeth.
It is well waullyd, and by estimation it is about a mile in compas.
There be in the waulls 5 gates. Brode-Gate, and that leadythe to Brode Strete, the fayrest parte of the towne. Olde Gate is alsoe toward Temde, as Brod-Gate is, but no so nere. Galfride Gate, Corve Gate toward the left ripe of Corve river, Mil-Gate. The castle hemithe in one parte of the towne and stondithe on a stronge rokke well dichid betwixte Corve-Gate and Mille-Gate. (The castle the west parte, Mortimers and the Duke of Yorke lords of it. Lady Geneville Mortimers wyfe.)[3]
There is but one paroche churche in the towne, but that is very faire, and large and richely adornyd, and taken for the fayrest in all those quarters. It stondithe even in the middle of the towne, and is in the highest ground of it.

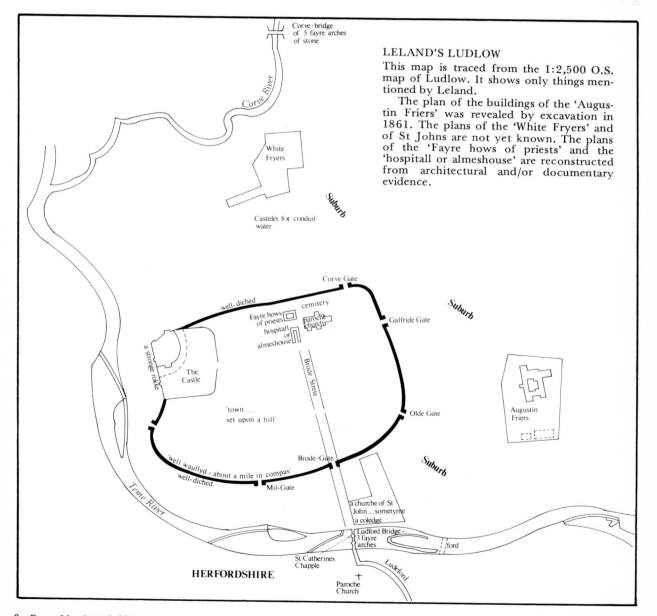

LELAND'S LUDLOW

This map is traced from the 1:2,500 O.S. map of Ludlow. It shows only things mentioned by Leland.

The plan of the buildings of the 'Augustin Friers' was revealed by excavation in 1861. The plans of the 'White Fryers' and of St Johns are not yet known. The plans of the 'Fayre hows of priests' and the 'hospitall or almeshouse' are reconstructed from architectural and/or documentary evidence.

3. Roger Mortimer (1287-1330) obtained a moiety of Ludlow by marrying Joan Geneville, great-great-grand-daughter of Walter Lacy (Eyton, p. 279). Richard Duke of York (1411-60), son of Anne Mortimer, inherited the Castle and a moiety of the manor in 1425 (Moir, p. 10).

*Part of the 'fayr hows' or college of the priests of the Palmers' Guild, seen from behind the* Rose and Crown. *An external chimney stack and two blocked-up windows can be seen. Two priests shared a heated living room but each had his own unheated sleeping chamber. The building was later a private house and became a Hospital in 1884.*

Thise churche hathe been muche avauncyd by a brothar-hode therein foundyd in the name of St. John the Evangeliste.[4] The originall thereof was as the people say there in the tyme of K.Edward the Confessor; and it is constantly afirmyd there that the pilgrimes, that browght the ringe from beyond the se as a token from St. John thevangelist to Kynge Edward, were inhabitaunts of Ludlow.

This fraternitie hathe a gardian chosen yerely amonge the burgesses, and to this college longe now a tenne pristes, partly found by endowment of lands, partly by gatheringe the devotion of the people thereabout. These priests have a fayr hows at the west end of the paroche church yard; and by it an hospitall or almeshouse of a 30 pore folks sometyme, and sometyme mo, amyntayned partly by the fraeternitie and partly by mony given for obiits of men buried there in the church.

There was a very rich merchant in Ludlowe not long synce called Hosier, buried in the parish church, who founded a cantarie in a part of the aforesaid colledge, endowing it with 10. or 12. £. land by the yeare. The stipend is now geven to a schoole-maister.[5]

*The White Conduit in the Bull Ring behind the Tolsey, as sketched by Ziegler in the 1820s (see p. 96). This was one of the 'castelets for conduit water' seen by Leland; the other was probably in Corve Street, just south of the present entrance to Station Drive. The water came from a spring at St Julian's well in Livesey Road.*

4. See pp. 26-7.
5. John Hosier died in 1463 (PRO: Prob. 11/5 f.1). The almshouses were in existence by 1482 and in 1486 his executors conveyed lands to the Palmers' Guild as a permanent endowment (*VCH* ii, p. 108).

The town-waule enclosethe the northe syde of the cemitery of the paroche churche. I noted these graves of men of fame in the church of Ludlowe.

Beaupie, somtyme coferer to Edward the 4. He geveth a leg in his armes.[6] } buried in the body
Cokkis, a gentleman servitor to Prince Arthur. } of the church

Doctor Denton, Master of St. John's in Ludlow. } buried in the
. . . Sulyard, justicier in the Marchis of Wales. } presbyterie

There be 2 castelets for conduit water in the towne, servyd bothe from one springe or head.[7]

There were 2. fayre coleges of friers in Ludlow. The Whit-Fryers was a fayre and costly thing and stood without Corve-Gate by north, almoste at the end of that suburbe. One . . . Ludelaw, a knight, lord of Stoke-castle or pile towards Bysshops-castle, was originall fownder there. Vernon by an heire generall is now owner of Stoke, and of late was taken as founder of this howse.[8]

The Augustin Friers stode without Galdford-Gate.[9]

I saw suburbes without all the gates of Ludlowe, savinge that I was not at Mill-gate. The suburbe over Temede bridge by southe is caullyd Ludeford, and in it is a little paroche churche.

There is on the northe syde of the bridge in ripa sinistra Temede, a churche of St. John standinge without Brode-Gate, sometyme a coledge with a dene and fellows of one Jourdann's foundation. There be 3 fayre arches in this bridge over Temde and a praty chapple apon it of St. Catherine.[10] It is but about 100 yeres syns this stone bridge was erectyd. Men passed afore by a ford a lytle benethe the bridge (. . . a ford a flite shot lower).[11]

Passynge out of Ludlow by Corve-gate I cam strayte to Corve-bridge of 5. fayre arches of stone. This Corve ryver goithe from this bridge strayte down by the castle of Ludlaw and a little benethe it goith into Teamd by the left ripe.

*(Left) A detail of the 1722 panorama of Ludlow (see pp. 62-3), showing the chapel of St Catherine on Ludford Bridge. The chapel was here by 1407, when Robert Mascall, Bishop of Hereford, granted 40 days indulgence to all who gave materials for its repair.*

*(Above) A thick wall of one of the buildings of the 'Whit-Fryers' or Carmelites, as revealed in a trial excavation by Birmingham University Archaeological Field Unit in October 1983. The friary was founded in 1350, just after the Black Death, and dissolved in 1538, two or three years before Leland's visit.*

6. Piers Beaupie was Member of Parliament for Ludlow 1472-75 (Weyman, 1895, p. 7). By his will, proved in 1480, he established a chantry in Ludlow Parish Church (PRO: Prob. 11/6 fo. 38).
7. Ludlow had a piped water supply as early as the mid-13th century.
8. *VCH* ii, pp. 93-95.
9. Ibid, pp. 95-96.
10. Ludford Bridge has been described architecturally as 'of the 15th century' (Pevsner, p. 188), but there was an earlier bridge on the site from at least the early 13th century (Lloyd, 1979, p. 10).
11. An 'arrow flight' was about 200 yards.

This is the earliest known map of any part of the Ludlow district, with the exception of Saxton's county map of Shropshire, which was printed the same year.[1] It was made for Edmund Walter (d.1593), an able lawyer practising at the bar of the Council of the Marches at Ludlow Castle, who later became Chief Justice of South Wales.[2] Walter, a native of Staffordshire, arrived in Ludlow in the 1560s and soon acquired five burgages in Broad Street, where he built 'a fayre house' (see p. 64). By 1577 he was rich enough to acquire property outside the town and commissioned this map to show its distribution.

Although the orientation is not always accurate, the map gives a revealing picture of the locality. It covers the hill country south, south-west and west of Ludlow, much of which is now known to geologists as 'the Ludlow anticline'. The highest areas, now Forestry Commission plantations, were then 'the Vallet wood of the Lordship of Richards Castle', while the felled tree trunks show that lumbering was already important. The 'water of Teame' is clearly marked on the left, with buildings of Ludlow on the north bank. On the south bank are 'Whitclyffe' the town's common land, and 'Foxes Land', i.e. Oakly Park, a hunting reservation acquired from the Crown by Charles Fox (d.1590), Secretary to the Council of the Marches. Along the bottom of the map is a much larger hunting area still held by the Crown, 'Bryngwoode Chase', which is separated from a line of enclosed fields by a prominently marked 'dyche and hedge'. Bringewood Chase supplied fuel and building materials for Ludlow Castle and a lease of 1601 shows that parts of it were leased to the Walter family.

*This photograph by Walter Harper, the Broad Street photographer, shows the tomb of Edmund Walter (d.1593) and Mary his wife (d.1583) in the chancel of the Parish Church. It was not erected until after 1625, when the cost was provided for in the will of James Walter, the eldest son. This lapse of time accounts for 1592 being wrongly given as the year of Edmund's death. James was M.P. for Radnor and lived at 'the Moor' in Richards Castle, which had been bought by his father and is clearly marked on the 1577 map.*

*The tomb is of alabaster and is entirely classical, with a profusion of detail which approaches the baroque. There are columns with Corinthian capitals, the back wall has an ornamented arch wreathed with 'antics', while above the entablature a cartouche incorporates the family coat of arms. The railings are of rust-free haematite iron from Cumberland. The photograph gives a fine view of the effigies, both of which are in Elizabethan dress.*

*The Walters are of interest as one of the leading Puritan families in the district. James Walter left bequests to Sir Robert Harley of Brampton Bryan, another Puritan, and to the Preacher of Richards Castle, who was Robert Horne, a well-known Puritan writer and Divine who was living in Ludlow. The second son, John, had a very successful legal career, becoming Chief Baron of the Exchequer, but he used his position to suppress bull baiting, plays and Sunday sports and was the only judge to try to curb the political excesses of Charles I.*

1. PRO: LRRO/2966
2. Weyman, H., 'The Walters at Ludlow—an Elizabethan Plan', *T.S.A.S.*, 4th ser., vol.3 (1913), pp.263-73.

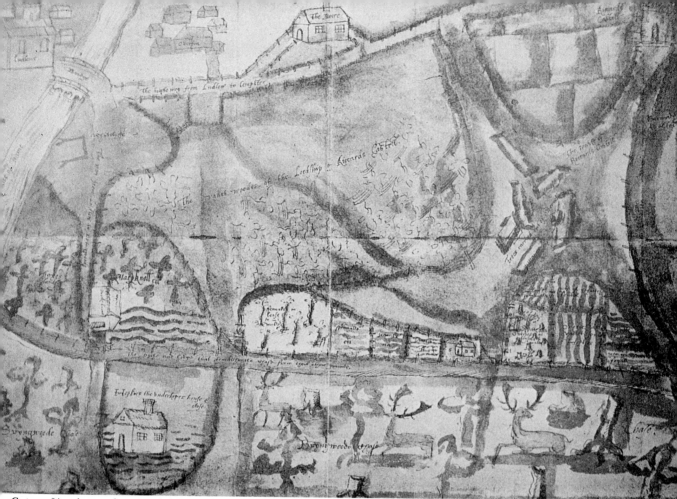

*Copy of 'a platte of parte of the Chase of Bryngwood and of certayne groundes leased to Mr. Walter of Ludlowe'.*

The top left hand corner of the 1577 map gives the earliest pictorial representation of any part of Ludlow, except for the conventional images in the windows of the Parish Church. Though the drawings are hastily done they are nevertheless of considerable historical interest.

Its relationship to 'Whitclyffe' and to 'the higheway' from 'Lempster' makes it clear that Ludford bridge is being shown. This would have been crossed by the Walters and their servants on journeys to and from the Moor. The width of the bridge has been exaggerated and the chapel of St Catherine omitted but the artist correctly shows the '3 fayre arches' noted by Leland some 35 years earlier (see p.36).

The church and the three small houses on the north bank may be conventional symbols for the town of Ludlow but Weyman argues cogently that the church is a drawing of the chapel of the Hospital of St John the Baptist, which stood on the bank of the river 'next to the bridge'. The Hospital was founded in the early 13th century, originally to give relief to the poor and infirm and hospitality to travellers, though by the 15th century it had become a small college of priests who served chantries in the Hospital chapel and at the Castle.[3] The chapel was built in the early 13th century, when the round-headed arches shown on the picture could still have been in use for such a building. though the spire was probably added later. The chapel is shown with two cells and is about the size which the small community would have required. Though the Hospital was effectively dissolved in 1539 the chapel was still in use in 1565 when it was part of the house built on the Hospital site by the Foxes of Ludford. There is no record of its demolition before 1636, when the stones were used to repair the wall of Ludlow churchyard.

3. *V.C.H.* 2, pp.102-3.

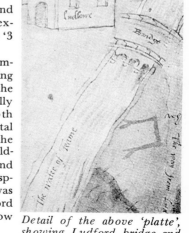

*Detail of the above 'platte', showing Ludford bridge and the chapel of the Hospital of St John the Baptist.*

William Camden (1551-1623) was a Londoner and a distinguished Oxford scholar. He taught at Westminster School, first as Second Master, then as Headmaster, though he found school-mastering 'laborious'.[1] He was also the most famous antiquarian scholar of his day. He became Clarenceux King of Arms at the College of Heralds, which has been described as 'the nearest thing in Elizabethan England to an Institute of Antiquarian Research'; and later founded a Chair of History at Oxford University.[2] The adoption of his name by the Camden Society, founded in 1838 to publish historical documents, shows how long his reputation has persisted.

Camden's best known work was *Brittania: A Chorographical description of the flourishing Kingdoms of England, Scotland and Ireland from the earliest antiquity.* The first edition, in Latin, was published in 1587 but it was translated in 1610, and there were revised versions in 1695, 1722 and 1772. Though Camden went on some journeys, e.g. to Wales in 1590, *Brittania* was based on what today would be called secondary sources, i.e. medieval chronicles and other documents, which Camden meticulously researched and copied. He went to great pains to widen his range of sources, e.g. he learnt Welsh so that he could read the Welsh chroniclers and understand Welsh place names; but his work lacks first-hand observation and he certainly did not visit many of the places described.

The Ludlow account reflects his use of the chronicles, indeed Matthew Paris (see p.15) is specifically mentioned in a side note. He is weak on local geography, e.g. he gives more attention to the Corve than to the Teme and confuses the circumference of the Castle with that of the town walls. Modern scholarship has shown that he was mistaken in attributing the foundation of the Castle to Roger de Montgomery; but the authority of 'the learned Camden' was so great that the error persisted until it was corrected by Eyton in 1854.[3] The most interesting comments are those on the Council of the Marches, which was at the height of its powers during Camden's lifetime. These were based on contemporary knowledge and reports rather than on written sources.

**Translation of the description of Ludlow in *Brittania*,** from the first Latin edition of 1587 (p. 386).
Additional text inserted in the 1695 edition by Edmund Gibson is bracketed.
Text omitted in the 1695 and other later editions is underlined.

*Next is Ludlow, in Welsh Dinan (and Lys-twysoc, that is, the Prince's Palace); it is seated on a hill where the Teme joins the Corve, a town of greater elegance than age. Roger de Montgomery first built a castle here which overlooks the Corve and from thence enclosed it with a wall about a mile in compass. Then, when his son Robert was banished, King Henry the First took it into his own hands and afterwards King Stephen's attack brought a siege which was pressed with great force; Henry, the son of the King of Scots, taken from his horse with an iron hook, was almost lost and almost dragged over the wall, but Stephen himself was on hand and with singular greatness of spirit rescued him from such danger. Afterwards King Henry the Second gave this castle with all the vale below it along the Corve, commonly called Corvedale, to Fulke de Dinan. Afterwards it belonged to the Lacys and through a daughter it descended to Geoffrey de Jeneville, of a Lorraine family, from whose posterity it descended, again by a daughter, to the Mortimers; and from them it came by inheritance into the sacred patrimony of the Prince. Afterwards the inhabitants erected a fair church upon the highest ground in the heart of the town, the only one they have; and from this time we may date its reputation and eminence beyond any of its neighbours. Though King Stephen, Simon de Montford and Henry the Sixth did much damage to it in several civil wars, yet it always recovered, more especially since King Henry the Eighth established the Council of the Marches, not unlike the French Parliaments; the Lord President whereof generally keeps his courts here which seldom slacken in business due to (the Sovereign Jurisdiction here exercised or) the litigious temper of the people (of Wales). This Council consists of a Lord President and as many Counsellors as the Prince (King) pleases, a Secretary, an Attorney, a Solicitor, and then four Justices of the Counties of Wales. Sir Henry Sidney now acts in the position of President, a most noble man and the most experienced of all antiquity, to whom succeeded Philip his son, a most famous knight, of whom I could not easily say what and how much Britain was consecrated by him; but snatched by an early death the sacred and heavenly assembly has now received him.*

1. *D.N.B.*
2. Piggot,S., Introduction to reprint of Camden's *Brittania*, p.6.
3. Eyton, pp.235-6; Hodges, in the first *History of Ludlow Castle* (1794), closely follows Camden, e.g. his statement that 'the town of Ludlow was anciently called by the Welsh Dinan', p.2.

# SIR HENRY SIDNEY
## AND HIS SON,
## SIR PHILIP SIDNEY, 1580s

Sir Henry Sidney (1529-86), Lord President of the Council in the Marches from 1560-86, is one of the best known holders of that office, though he was only regularly in the Marches between 1571 and 1575.[1] At other times he was at court or in Ireland, where he was three times Lord Deputy. He enjoyed his work in Wales, writing to Sir Francis Walsingham in 1583:

> *A happie place of government it is, for a better people to govern and better subjects to their soveraign Europe holdeth not.*[2]

His son Philip (1554-86), who spent short periods of his boyhood at Ludlow Castle, has become the personification of the talented and versatile Elizabethan. He was greatly admired in his own lifetime whilst his heroic death at Zutphen, attacking the hated Spaniards, brought him the sort of posthumous adulation given to John Kennedy in 1963. Camden's comments, written very soon after Sir Philip's death, reflect these sentiments. He wrote a number of poems and other works but there is nothing to connect any of these with Ludlow.

*Monument to Ambrosia Sidney, aged 14, Sir Henry's fourth daughter, who died at Ludlow Castle in 1574. It is a simple tomb chest, let into the ribbing of the chancel of the Parish Church. Sir Henry's own heart was buried at Ludlow but no memorial was erected.*

*This photograph, taken before 1884, shows the large building in King Street once known as Kingston's Place. An earlier structure, leased from the Corporation, was rebuilt in 1576 by Thomas Hankey (d.1588), Steward of the Council of the Marches and probably a personal servant of Sir Henry Sidney. The ground floor shops were sub-let but the Hankeys lived on the upper floors. One of the rooms had an oak fireplace over which were the arms of Sir Henry Sidney. This shows how Council officials permeated the whole town, even here in the old Drapers' Row, Ludlow's commercial heart.*

1. Williams, p.252.
2. P.R.O. S.P.12, 159/1, dated 1 March, 1583.

Thomas Churchyard (1520-1604) was born in Shrewsbury, though his maternal grandfather was Thomas Cookes (d.1513) of Ludlow, gentleman servitor to Prince Arthur.[1] He had a versatility of talent shown by many Elizabethans. He was a widely travelled courtier and soldier, fighting many times in Flanders, e.g. in 1570 he was captured at Tergoas after 'greate service sondrie tymes' for the Prince of Orange against the Spaniards. He also wrote more than sixty books, though some of these were only leaflets or 'Epitaphes'.

The great part of *The Worthiness of Wales* is verse, written in ten-line stanzas, each of which finishes with a writing of 'what I have beheld and thoroughly seen'. He began in Monmouthshire and travelled north, giving particular attention to Ludlow; being the headquarters of the Council of the Marches 'it stands for Wales, most apt, most fit and best'. The book was published in 1587 but was written at least a year before, for a sidenote implies that Sir Henry Sidney, who died in 1586, was still Lord President of the Council.

The great part of *The Worthiness of Wales* is verse, written in ten line stanzas, each of which finishes with a rhyming couplet. Much of it is doggerel but occasionally Churchyard produces a memorable line or phrase. The verse is often accompanied by informative sidenotes and is sometimes replaced by prose.

There are some 250 lines of Ludlow, arranged in three separate poems. The first poem, called 'Ludloe Towne, Church and Castle' has seven stanzas but the references to the castle are only incidental. The second poem is 'The Castle of Ludloe' which has three descriptive stanzas and some short prose passages and includes a long list of arms in the building now known as the Round Chapel. It is interesting that the list begins with Sir Walter Lacy, whom Churchyard describes as 'first owner of Ludloe castle'.[2] The third poem is called 'The Towne of Ludloe and many good gifts graunted to the same'.

The first verse of 'Lodloe Towne, Church and Castle' is one of the best written by Churchyard and has often been quoted by later writers:

*The names of streates there, Castle streate, Broad streate, Old streate, And the Mill streate.*

*A fayre house by the gate of the making of Justice Walter.[3]*

'*The towne doth stand most part upon an hill,*
*Built well and fayre, with streates both large and wide,*
*The houses such, where straungers lodge at will,*
*As long as there the councell lists abide,*
*Both fine and cleane the streates are all throughout,*
*With conduits cleere, and wholesome water springs;*
*And who that lists to walke the towne about,*
*Shall finde therein some rare and pleasant things;*
*But chiefly there the ayre so sweet you have,*
*As in no place ye can no better crave.*'

The first six lines of the second verse, though less well written, are also of great interest. With the side notes they give the best description we have of Elizabethan Castle Street, with its market house and 'fayre houses' on 'every side'. The 'fayre house of Maister Sackford' is now Castle Lodge and the house 'that Maister Secretarie Fox did bestowe great charges on' was around what is now Quality Square.[4]

*Next this is a fayre house of Maister Sack- fords which he did buyld, and a fayre house that Maister Secretarie Fox did bestowe greate charges on.*

'*The market house, where corne and oates are sold,*
*Is covered ore, and kept in finest sort;*
*From which ye shall, the castle well behold,*
*And to which walke, doe many men resort.*
*On every side thereof fayre houses are,*
*That makes a shew, to please both mynd and eye:*'

1. Adnitt, H. W., 'Thomas Churchyard', *T.S.A.S.*, vol. iii (1880), pp. 1-68.
2. Walter Lacy (d.1085) was the father of Roger Lacy, probably the founder of Ludlow Castle.
3. Nos. 35-37 Broad Street. This and other houses identified from the Ludlow Corporation Burgage rental of 1619 (S.R.O. 356, box 400) and other sources. Edmund Walter (d.1593) was Chief Justice of South Wales (see p. 38).
4. Thomas Sackford was Porter and Keeper of the Prisons in the Marches of Wales (Weyman, 1913, p. 90). Charles Fox (d.1590) was Secretary to the Council of the Marches (Weyman, 1895, pp. 10-11).

In 'The Town of Ludloe and many good Gifts etc. . .' Churchyard gives us glimpses of various aspects of town life, confirming what can be learnt from documents. He outlines the government of the town:

> *'Two bayliefs rule, one yeere the towne throughout,*
> *Twelve aldermen they have therein likewise'*[5]

There are details of the church services:

> *'Three tymes a day in church good service is,*
> *At six o'clocke, at nine, and then at three'*

The fairs and markets, then as always, were the lifeblood of the town:

> *'Two fayres a yeere, they have on severall daies,*
> *Three markets kept, but Monday chiefe I troe'*[6]

*The interior of Quality Square, which preserves the courtyard plan of 'the fayre house' of Secretarie Fox. The house occupied two former burgages, each 49½ ft. wide, i.e. 3 poles. Parts of it were in brick, a rare building material in Ludlow at this time; and small, irregular bricks, embedded in thick mortar, can be seen in the top right hand corner. The house was divided into several small properties in the late 17th century but the name 'Quality' recalls its former splendour.*

*(Below) Castle Lodge, the 'fayre house' of Maister Sackford. The stone parts were built by Sackford in the 1580s, combining three former properties. The timber framed upper storey was added a few years later, probably when it was the residence of Robert Berry, an influential official of the Council of the Marches and Ludlow's Member of Parliament.*

5. See pp. 86-7.
6. The fairs were on the 9th, 10th (St Laurence's Day) and 11th of August and the 24th, 25th (St Katherine's Day) and 26th of November. The May fair, granted in the 1461 charter, had been discontinued by 1552 and was not revived until the 1820s (see p. 86).

Daniel Powell was the eldest son of David Powell, D.D. (1552-1598), a 16th-century historian of Wales. He was present in Ludlow on 4 November 1616, perhaps because he held some minor appointment at the Council of the Marches. He was, he tells us, 'not altogether an idle Actor nor unwilling Spectator' at a 'solemnity' held in the town to mark 'the Creation of the high and mighty Charles, Prince of Wales and Earle of Chester, In his Maiesties Palace of Whitehall'. He was, he continues, 'so ravished with the fullness of joy' which he saw 'in the hearts of the people' that he wished to be 'transformed into the shape of the sweet Nightingale', so that he could describe the day's events 'to the eares of all men'. The work, called *The Love of Wales to their souveraigne Prince*, was finished within the month, for the preamble is dated 'From Ludlow this last of November 1616'; and before the end of the year it had been printed by Nicholas Okes of London. It was reprinted in 1841 by the Hon. R. H. Clive of Oakly Park in his *Documents connected with the History of Ludlow and the Lord Marchers.*[1]

The 'solemnity' at Ludlow on 4 November 1616 was a major propaganda exercise by the government of King James I, who was not enjoying much popularity at the time. There had been a similar ceremony at Chester in 1610 when James' eldest son, Henry, was created Prince of Wales. Henry, unlike his father, was very popular, especially with Protestants, and his premature death in 1612 was widely lamented. The events of 1616 were an attempt to give the rather haughty Charles the sort of popular appeal enjoyed by his brother. There was an imposing ceremony in London itself, described in *Civitatis Amor: the Cities Love to Prince Charles* (1616), a similar tract to that written by Powell. Ludlow, the headquarters of the Council of the Marches, was singled out for a parallel ceremony, largely because of its current administrative importance but partly because of its historic links with earlier Princes of Wales.

Some of the most important Counsellors of Wales and the Marches were ordered to attend the investiture in Whitehall; and as so often the President, Ralph Lord Eure, was absent from Ludlow. But it was 'by the appointment and direction' of the President that the solemnity in Ludlow was organised. The chief dignitary was Sir Thomas Chamberlaine (d.1625), Knight, Sergeant at Law and Chief Justice of Chester, and he was attended by Sir Thomas Cornewalle (1538-1623) of Burford, High Sheriff of Shropshire and many other Counsellors and 'worthy Gentlemen and persons of good account of the Counties of Salop, Hereford, Denbigh, Mountgomery, Caernarvon, Merionith and other Counties adjoyning, to the number of many thousand persons'.

As in all propaganda exercises publicity was the first priority. Powell begins his account:

> *First the said Justice commanded that our said prince his Armes, with his Name, and Stile there-under in Characters fairely subscribed, should be set up and published, as well under the Pulpit in the Church of Saint Laurence in Ludlow, and in his Maiesties Chappell within the said Castle, and in the Court-house of the Principalitie there, as also upon the gates of the said Towne, and high Crosses there, and likewise upon the principall Posts and Pillars standing in the Market place within the said Towne of Ludlow.*
>
> *The tenour of which Stile and Subscription here issueth.*
>
> *Quarto Nouembris. Annon Dom. 1616*
>
> 'The right, high, Mighty and excellent Prince Charles, Prince of great Britaine and Ireland, Duke of Cornewall, Yorke-and of Albany, Marquesse of Ormont, Earle of Rosse, Baron of Armanoch, of the most noble order of the Garter Knight, Second Sonne by Birth, and now the only and first begotten Sonne of the most puissant and potent James by the Grace of God, of England, Scotland, France and Ireland King, is this day at White-Hall created Prince of Wales, and Earle of Chester; and here at Ludlow by us of the Counsell solemnized within the said Principalitie of Wales.'

The events of the day were described in great detail by Powell and even allowing for some exaggeration, the scale of the celebration is impressive. The main purpose of the 'solemnity' was to impress the Creation of the Prince of Wales on the minds of his subjects but the ceremonies devised also symbolise the association between the Council of the Marches and the Borough of Ludlow. For economic and social reasons the burgesses were anxious to have the Council in their midst and as recently as 1613 a collection had been made in the Borough to raise the means for persuading the Council to spend the next law term in Ludlow.[2]

1. pp.58-80
2. Williams,P., 'Government and Politics in Ludlow, 1590-1642', *T.S.A.S.*, vol.56, p.282

Eight main phases of the ceremony can be distinguished, as summarised below:

1. The procession of the Bailiffs to the Castle.
   *About nine of the clocke in the fore-noon . . . William Gregory and Thomas Blashfield Esquires, Bailifes of the said Towne . . . accompanied with the Magistrates their Brethren and all the chiefe Burgesses, very richly clad and apparrelled, attended by their Officers with their Maces and all the Quire of the Church there, singing of Hymnes and Psalms, bringing with them sixe yong Youths of the Kings free Schoole well and richly decked who did bear in their hands severall Penons and Bannerolls of the Arms and Atchivements of our said Prince Charles . . . Having before them the Towne Waites and other lowd Instruments of Musicke marched along the number of two hundred souldiers with Halberds, Pikes, Corslets, Muskets and Caliuers . . . came up to the Castle to attend and bring the said Justice and Counsell to the Church.*

2. The return procession to the Church with Maister Justice.
   *And having repaired to the Castle Green . . . and meeting Maister Justice in his Scarlet Robes, with the rest of the Counsell . . . accompanied with all the worshipfull Counsellors of Law, Atturnies and Clarks with sundry Esquires and Gentlemen . . . together with all the chiefe Officers of the said Castle . . . and having another company of Waits and good consorts of Musicke . . . a great Volley of Shot was fired which so pierced the Ayre with the great noyse of Drummes and sound of Trumpets, Fifes, Flutes and other Instruments, as the like in these parts hath not been seene . . . and marshalling themselves in good array they all went through the Towne Streets to the Church.*

3. The service in the Parish Church.
   *After Prayers said, and Psalms sung, one M. Thomas Pierson, a grave reverend divine and worthy Preacher, made a very learned sermon of an houre and halfe long.*

4. The proclamation at the High Cross by six scholars of the Free School (all of them the sons of members of the Corporation).
   *And as they issued out of the Church and Churchyard into the Market place, there was a new Scaffolde purposely erected neare unto the high Crosse . . . upon which . . . the said Schollers with their Penons . . . in their hands ascended; and as the said Justice and Counsell passed by . . . uttered and pronounced . . . severall Speeches . . . All of which were principally invented and made by the painfull industrie of . . . Humfrey Herbert Chiefe Schoolemaister of His Maiesties Free Schoole there . . .*

5. Return to the Castle and the proclamation by the Justice.
   *The which Speeches being ended . . . they marched and passed by sundry . . . great bonfires . . . and there marching, discharging of shot, singing, playing on instruments and heartily rejoicing, proceeded into the Court-house of the said Principalitie . . . where the said Justice . . . in the presence of the whole Company there . . . delivered these words . . . 'This happy and glorious day . . . being the first . . . of our Terme . . . The High and Mighty Prince Charles . . . Second Sonne by birth and now the Onely and First Begotten Sonne of the most potent . . . James . . . is this day at his Maiesties Palace of White-hall created Prince of Wales and Earle of Chester, being the thirteenth prince by Creation, in succession of his Noble Principalitie of Wales . . .' And thereupon all the Musick played . . . and another piercing and thundring Volley of shot was let flie . . .*

6. The Council and the Corporation dine separately.
   *And then, being full one of the clocke in the afternoone, the said Justice and Counsell, with the Knights, Esquires and best sort of Gentlemen returned into the Castle to dinner where was a great Feast provided . . . the Bailiffes also with their Brethren and Burgesses went downe to the Towne, to spend the rest of the day in all joyfull and joviall manner . . . having all drunke plentifully of wine by appointment of . . . chiefe Steward to the Kings Household there . . .*

7. Evening service at the Castle.
   *Dinner being scarce ended in the Castle the . . . Bailiffs in like pompe, beinge againe accompanied with the whole Quire of the Church . . . came up with great solemnitie into the Castle where Maister Justice joyfully receiving them, brought them straight into the Chappell there to offer their Evening Sacrifice . . . which being finished the aforesaid Schollers very humbly prostrating themselves . . . delivered up their sayd severall Banerolls into the hands of the said Justice.*

8. Further ceremonies of 5 November.
   *The Bailiffes . . . humbly taking their leave . . . Maister Justice required them . . . to express their joy . . . for our said Soveraignes . . . Deliverance . . . from the Papists treasonable and horrible conspiracie . . . and to be in readiness with the . . . Justice and Counsell the next morning . . . to praise God for the same . . . Which accordingly was performed the next day . . . the Musicke, Ringing and Bonefires continuing . . . all the said day.*

John Milton (1608-74) was a major English poet who also wrote on behalf of Parliament during the Civil War and Commonwealth. His early works include *A Maske Represented before the right ho'ble the Earl of Bridgewater Lord President of Wales . . . At Ludlow Castle the 29th. of September 1634.*[1] This masque, later known as *Comus*, is the best known literary work closely associated with Ludlow. It is a rare survival from the 'grand occasions' often held at the Castle at this time, e.g. the 'solemnity' at Ludlow . . . on 4 November 1616 when Charles was created Prince of Wales in Whitehall.[2]

John Egerton (1579-1649), Earl of Bridgewater, was a distinguished soldier and Privy Councillor. In 1631 his service was rewarded by the Presidency of the Council of the Marches but like other holders of that office he delegated much of the work. He did not come to the Welsh border until 1634 when he arrived in Ludlow in early July and left in October, though for much of the intervening period he was on a tour to Cheshire.[3] The masque was presented near the end of the Visitation, as part of a formal occasion at Ludlow Castle on Michaelmas night. Michaelmas, like other quarter days, was then an important religious and folk festival and was often used for inaugurations.[4] No contemporary account of the occasion has survived but a manuscript of the antiquarian William Oldys (1696-1761) testifies that 'a large concourse of the neighbouring nobility and gentry' were in attendance;[5] while it is likely that the Bailiffs of Ludlow, Edward Colbach, corviser, and Thomas Crowther, mercer, were also present, as their predecessors had been in 1616.

A masque has been defined as 'a dramatic entertainment involving dances and disguises, in which spectacle and music predominate over plot and character'.[6] Masques were popular at Court and among the nobility. *A Maske . . . at Ludlow* has less spectacle than the true court masque and some would see it as 'a pastoral entertainment', with some of the features of a medieval morality play. There is general agreement that it was written 'for a special occasion by a specific group of actors'.[7] Milton probably got the commission through Henry Lawes (1596-1662), music tutor to the Egerton family, who wrote at least some of the music himself. They had collaborated in 1632 to produce *Arcades* for the Earl's mother-in-law, the Countess of Derby, who lived at Harefield in Hertfordshire, close to Milton's study retreat at Horton in Buckinghamshire and to the Egerton family home at Ashridge.[8] He was also known to the Egertons in other ways, e.g. one of their doctors was Theodore Diodati, who was the father of Charles Diodati, Milton's closest friend.

The plot revolves round the three children of the Earl who are lost in 'a dreer wood' as they travel to Ludlow. These parts were actually played by three of the Earl's 15 children: Lady Alice, aged 15; Lord Brackley, aged 13; and Mr. Thomas Egerton, aged 9. The masque gave them an opportunity to display their learning and acting skills 'for the pleasure and pride of their parents' and for the gratification of their tutor, who himself played the Attendant Spirit.[9] The Lady is separated from her brothers and waylaid by Comus, a magician who tempts travellers to drink a liquor which makes them half-beasts and enslaves them in his rabble rout. In the central dramatic dialogue of the masque the Lady resists temptation until the brothers, helped by the Attendant Spirit, rush in and disperse Comus and his rabble; but the Lady can only be released from her enchanted chair by Sabrina, goddess of the Severn. Masques conventionally celebrated the triumph of virtue and this had special point for the Egertons, for in 1631 their relative, the Earl of Castlehaven, had been the central figure of a notorious sexual scandal.[10]

It is unlikely that Milton saw the 1634 performance or ever came to Ludlow. There is a tradition that the Bridgewater children were lost in Haywood forest, some three miles south of Ludlow and local guidebooks even locate

1.  Quotations from the text are taken from the Bridgewater manuscript, reproduced in Sprott,S.E. (Ed.), *John Milton: A Maske. The Earlier Versions.* (Toronto, 1973).
2.  See p.44-5.
3.  Inf. ex. Mr. C.Brown, Senior Lecturer, Reading University.
4.  Hunter,W.B., 'The Liturgical Context of Comus', *English Language Notes*, Sept. 1972, pp.11-3.
5.  Warton,T., *Poems . . . by John Milton* (1785), p.133.
6.  Harvey,P. (Ed.), *The Oxford Companion to English Literature* (3rd. ed., 1946), p.504.
7.  Diekhoff,J.S., *A Maske at Ludlow* (1968), p.15.
8.  Hill,C., *Milton and the English Revolution* (1977), pp.43-4.
9.  Diekhoff, op. cit., p.3.
10. Breasted,B., 'Comus and the Castlehaven Scandal', *Milton Studies*, 3 (1971), pp.201-4.

the incident in Sunny Gutter, sometimes called 'Comus Valley'.[11] Unfortunately none of this can be substantiated, and it is more probable that literary sources suggested the plot, e.g. medieval Advent plays, where 'the lady wandering in the Wilderness', pictured in *Revelation* 12, is rescued from Antichrist by the Archangel Michael.[12]

The theme of the masque is universal but it is located in time and place, as part of the tradition of flattering the patron, in this case the Earl of Bridgewater. Comus's claim that he had seen the brothers:

> . . . *what tyme the labour'd oxe/in his loose traces from the furrowe came,/and the swink't hedger at his supper sate* (291-3)

and his affected knowledge of the wood:

> *I know each lane, and every Alley greene,/Dingle, or bushie dell, of this wide wood, And everie boskie bourne from side to side/my daylie walks and antient neighbourhood* (311-4)

evoke pleasing pictures of the countryside south of Ludlow; but they describe other parts of 17th century England just as well. Only two passages are of particular local interest, showing how the Welsh borderland was perceived by Milton, probably writing in far away Buckinghamshire.

Early in the masque Milton flatters the Earl and describes the character of Wales:

> *and all this tract that fronts the fallinge sunn/a noble Peer of mickle trust and power/has in his Chardge, with tempred awe to guyde/an ould and haughty nacon, proud in armes* (53-6)

There is a more specific reference in the last scene, described as 'Ludlowe and the Presidents Castle':

> *where this night are met in state/ many a friend to gratulate/his wish't presence, and beside/All the swaynes that nere abide/With Iiggs and rurall daunce resort,/wee shall catch them at this sport* (902-7)

Milton, brought up in London and Cambridge, makes Ludlow seem more rustic and provincial than it was but the jigs of his swains are an important dramatic device, for they provide a joyful but legitimate alternative to the bacchanalian romps of Comus's rabble. Moreover, the gathering is a fitting audience for the Attendant Spirit's final message, the concluding moral of the masque:

> *Mortalls that would follow me/love vertue, she alone is free,/she can teach you how to clyme/higher than the spherie chime/or if vertue feeble were/Heven it selfe would stoope to her* (943-8)

A slightly revised version of the original text was printed in 1637 but in the years after the Restoration this message, and in fact Milton's work generally, did not match the mood of the times and *The Maske* was ignored by visitors to Ludlow such as Dineley, Defoe and Stukeley. In 1737 an adaptation for the London stage was called *Comus* but though this title was used when the 1637 version was reprinted in 1747, *A Mask presented at Ludlow . . .* was retained as a sub-title, so that as the work became popular its association with Ludlow was also widely known.[13] In 1785 Thomas Warton, an Oxford don, published a new edition of Milton's earlier poems, in which *Comus* is accompanied by a description of Ludlow Castle, visited by Warton on one of his archaeological tours. Subsequently, the 'celebrated Masque of Comus' was mentioned by nearly all the many travel-writers who visited the town. In the 20th century there have been revivals in the Castle in 1934 and in the 1950s while another is planned for 1984, the 350th anniversary of the first performance.

11. Baker,O., *Ludlow: Town and Neighbourhood* (1906), p.76.
12. Scoufos,A., 'The Mysteries in Milton's Masque', *Milton Studies*, 6 (1974), p.113.
13. B.L. catalogue.

Richard Baxter (1615-91) was a nonconformist divine who was born at Eaton Constantine, near Shrewsbury. His association with Ludlow is explained in the extract below, taken from *Reliquiae Baxterianae*, published in 1696.

From 1640 to 1660 Baxter was associated with Kidderminster, where he is remembered as the founder of the Ind-
ependent Church.[1] He was a Parliamentary chaplain during the Civil War but supported the Restoration. He became
a well known preacher and writer but was often in conflict with the established church, being imprisoned in 1685-6
and fined by Judge Jefferies on the charge of libelling the church.

> *When I was ready for the University my Master drew me into another way which kept me thence, where were
> my vehement desires. He had a friend at Ludlow, Chaplain to the Council there, called Mr. Richard Wickstead;
> whose place having allowance from the king (who maintaineth the House) for one to attend him, he told my
> master that he was purposed to have a Scholar fit for the University; and having had but one, would be better to
> him than any Tutor in the University would be; whereupon my Master persuaded me to accept the offer, and told
> me it would be better than the University to me. I believed him as knowing no better my self; and it suited well
> with my Parents minds, who were willing to have me as near to them as possible (having no Children but myself):
> And so I left my Schoolmaster for a supposed Tutor. But when I had tried him I found my self deceived: his
> business was to please the Great Ones and seek Preferment in the World; and to that end found it necessary some-
> times to give the Puritans a flirt; and call them unlearned, and speak much for Learning, being but a Superficial
> Scholar of himself. He never read to me, nor used any savoury Discourse of Godliness; only he loved me, and
> allowed me Books and Time enough: So that I as I had no considerable helps from him in my Studies so had I now
> considerable hindrance.*
>
> *And though the house was great (there being four Judges, the King's Attorney, the Secretary, the Clerk of the
> Fines with all their Servants, and all the Lord President's Servants and many more) and though the town was full
> of Temptations, through the multitude of persons (councillors, attorneys, officers and clerks), and much given to
> tippling and excess, it pleased God not only to keep me from them, but also to give me one intimate Companion,
> who was the greatest help to my Seriousness in religion than ever I had before and was a daily watchman over my
> soul . . .*
>
> *From Ludlow Castle, after a year and a half, I returned to my father's house . . . After that Mr. Francis Garbett
> (the faithful, learned minister at Wroxeter) for about a month read logic to me . . .*

Later Baxter recalls an incident when he played at dice and won against the odds, making him think the devil was
enticing him 'to be a gamester', with the result that he resolved to 'never more play at tables'. The description begins:

> *About seventeen years of age, being at Ludlow Castle where many idle gentlemen had little else to do, I had a
> mind to learn to play at Tables, and the best gamester in the house undertook to teach me . . .*

*This imposing timber framed building, No.45 Bull Ring, had become the* Bear Inn *by
the early 1630s, when the landlord was Thomas Hitchcox (d.1644). It may have been
known to Baxter, for Hitchcox was one of a small but influential circle of Ludlow
Puritans. These Puritans, mostly tradesmen, were in touch with local gentry like the
Harleys (see p.49) and the Walters, but for spiritual leadership they probably looked
to the Rev. Robert Horne (d.1640), a well known preacher and divine who lived at
what is now No.1 Broad Street. When Hitchcox died he bequeathed his soul to
Almighty God trusting 'to be one of His elect' and an inheritor of 'the kingdome of
heaven . . .'*[4]

1. *D.N.B.*
2. In 1626 recognisances to sell beer or ale were granted to over 100 Ludlow residents but only 16 of these had inns known by their
   signs. These were (modern postal numbers in brackets): *Anchor* (28-30 Broad Street), *Angel* (9 Broad Street), *Antyloppe* (49
   Broad Street), *Bell* (21 Bell Lane), *Bull* (14 Bull Ring), *Cross Keys* (Church Inn), *Crown* (56-58 Broad Street), *Falcon* (52 Broad
   Street), *George* (8 High Street), *Green Dragon* (9 Corve Street), *Gryffyn* (23 Bull Ring), *Harp* (102 Corve Street), *Red Lyon*
   (3 Old Street/13 Tower Street), *Rose and Crown* (145 Corve Street), *Star* (24-25 Broad Street), *Talbot* (139 Corve Street).
3. Francis Garbutt (c.1578-?) was an old boy of Ludlow Grammar School (Lloyd, 1977, pp.45,52).
4. HRO AA/20 1644: No.86.

These letters were written by Brilliana Harley (c.1600-43), the third wife of Sir Robert Harley of Brampton Bryan, 11 miles west of Ludlow, where the Harleys had been established for generations. Sir Robert Harley (1579-1658) was a zealous Puritan and energetically supported Parliament in the Civil War. The letters were all written to Edward Harley (1624-1700), Brilliana's son, who was resident at Oxford for the academic years 1638-9 and 1639-40 and then joined his father in London, later captaining a troop in the Parliamentary army. The letters were published by the Camden Society in 1853. They provide varied and informative glimpses of life in Ludlow during the 1638-43 period.

p.13     Nov. 30th, 1638
*Your father was yesterday at Loudlow, where the caus was hard betwne Sr. Gillberd Cornewall and his sisters, and it went against Sr. Gillberd Cornewwell, to his shame*

[i.e. a case heard before the Council of the Marches]

p.86     March 14, 1639
*Ludlo haue made choise of Mr. Goodwin to be burgesse, hauing refused my lord president his letters for Sr. Robert Nepper, his son in law*

[This is a reference to the 1639 election for what was later called 'the Short Parliament'. Ralph Goodwyn, senior member for Ludlow in every Parliament since 1623, was a rich 'carpet-bagger' from Bristol. In 1639 he is said to have 'feasted the Burgesses and endeavours by their bellies to gain their tongues'.[1] ]

p.123    Apr: the first, 1641
*I send this letter by the post of Loudlow, whoo is newly seet up; if you will write by him weakeley, I will send, if pleas God, for the letters; for it will be eassyrer then to send to Shrewsbury*

p.125    Apr: 14, 1641
*I send this by the post of Hariford, becaus I know not weather the post of Loudlow euer deleured my letter or no*

p.172    Jne 24, 1642
*Mr. William Littleton being in Loudlow last weake, as he came out of the church, a man came to him and looked him in the face and cryed 'roundhead'; he gave the fellow a good box of the eare and steep to on that had a chugell and took it from him and beat him soundly. They say they are now more quiet in Loudlow*

p.174    Jun 27, 1642
*Heariford is growne now wors than Loudlowe*

p.200    May 9, 1643
*Petter is still in prison at Loudlow. 5 men set upon him; he fought very valiently with them all; they had Carrabins and pole axes*

p.202    June 11, 1643
*Honest Petter is come out of prison. He was Greeuiously used in Loudlow. Turkes could have used him no wors; a lefftenant coronell Marrow would come every day and kicke him up and downe, and they laied him in a dungon upon foule straw*

1. Weyman (1895), pp.24-25

A probate inventory is a list of 'the goods and chattels' of a deceased person which had to be exhibited when a will was proved or an administration granted. Ludlow inventories survive in significant numbers only from 1660 and as elsewhere they deteriorate in quality after 1740; but for the intervening 80 years they provide a vivid insight into the domestic and commercial life of the town.

The example given is part of a long inventory of 'Francis Clent, junior', who was buried on 17 December 1662, aged only 21.[1] Although in trade on his own account he seems to have shared the premises of his father, 'Mr. Francis Clent', who was landlord of the large *Red Lion Inn*, at what is now No. 3 Old Street.[2] He is described as 'haberdasher', but the small ware usually associated with that trade was valued at only £3 18s 4d, whereas 'hatts, bands and Lynnings' were worth £36 15s 9½d and dried fruits, spices, soap and tobacco, normally sold by mercers, were worth £10 18s 8d. With debts the inventory totalled only £66 16s 7½d, and is a long way short of the town's more substantial tradesmen, e.g. Tamberlaine Davies, mercer, assessed at £854 14s 4d in 1685; but it is of considerable interest because of the range of goods stocked and because of the way that it is arranged.[3]

As the extract shows most of the goods are listed under the suppliers from whom they were obtained. The dried fruits, sugars, spices and other exotic items came from Mr. Wooton and Mr. Deddicott, who were wholesale grocers at Bewdley, an important river port on the navigable Severn, some 20 miles east of Ludlow.[4] The range of the spices stocked by young Clent is particularly impressive. These were luxury items, many of them from the East and West Indies, and were needed to impart flavour and piquancy to preserved and often tasteless foods. The officials of the Council of the Marches, restored in 1660, and the gentry of the surrounding countryside, already using Ludlow as a social centre, provided a market for goods of this kind.

| Mr. Wootton and Mr. Deddicotts Wares | | | |
|---|---|---|---|
| Maligo Resings 3 q(ua)rters & 23 lbs at 28s p(er) Cwt | 01 | 06 | 09 |
| Res. Sol 18lb at 45s. p(er) Cwt | 00 | 08 | 01 |
| Second Currens - 22 lbs at 49s p(er) Cwt | 00 | 09 | 07½ |
| Refine Sug(er) - 30 lbs at 10d p(er) li | 01 | 05 | 00 |
| po(o)r Suger - 15 lbs ½ at 8½d p(er) lb | 00 | 10 | 07½ |
| Mevis Suger - 33 li ½ at 4d p(er) lb | 00 | 11 | 02 |
| Safron - one oz and ½ at 2s. 2d p(er) oz | 00 | 03 | 03 |
| Large Mace - 2 ozs ¾ at 10d p(er) oz | 00 | 02 | 03½ |
| Cloves - 14 ozs ½ at 10d p(er) lb | 00 | 12 | 01 |
| Nutte - 9 ozs zt 5s 10d p(er) li | 00 | 03 | 03½ |
| Synam(i)t - 6 ozs at 4d p(er) oz | 00 | 02 | 00 |
| Pepp(er) - 12 li ¼ at 14d p(er) li | 00 | 14 | 03½ |
| White pepp(er) - 5 ozs at | 00 | 00 | 06 |
| Large and ground giner 7lbs at 7d p(er) lb | 00 | 04 | 01 |
| Aneseede - 2 li ½ at 8d per lb | 00 | 01 | 08 |
| Wormseede ½ li at 4s 8d per li | 00 | 02 | 04 |
| Carraway seede 11 ozs at 7d p(er) li | 00 | 00 | 05 |
| Lycoris - 1 li 13 ozs at 6d p(er) lb | 00 | 00 | 11 |
| Culminseede - 7 ozs at 9d p(er) li | 00 | 00 | 04 |
| Bay berryee 1 li at | 00 | 00 | 06 |
| Grayne - 1 li 2 ozs at 6d p(er) li | 00 | 00 | 06½ |
| Turmerik - 13 ozs at 16d p(er) li | 00 | 01 | 01 |
| Galles - li 4 ozs at 10d p(er) li | 00 | 01 | 10½ |
| Brimston - 2 lbs 6 ozs at 3d p(er) lb | 00 | 00 | 07 |
| Corne po(o)r - 4 ozs at 12d p(er) li | 00 | 00 | 03 |
| Crowne sope - 18 li at 4½d p(er) li | 00 | 06 | 09 |
| London sope a firkin & 3 li at 15s 9d p(er) firkin | 00 | 16 | 07 |
| White starch - 5 li at 5d p(er) li | 00 | 02 | 03½ |
| po(o)r Blewe - 1 li at | 00 | 00 | 08 |
| Indico - ¾ oz at | 00 | 00 | 03 |
| Shott - 28 li at 17s p(er) Cwt | 00 | 04 | 03 |
| | 08 | 14 | 04* |

* The total should be £8 12s 8d.

1. HRO AA/20 1662.
2. SRO 356 box 472, various tax assessments for Old Street and Galdeford ward, 1650s, 1661; ibid, box 400, 1669 Corporation burgage rental.
3. HRO AA/20 box 105.
4. Inf. ex. Bewdley Historical Research Group.

John Ogilby (1600-76) was a Scotsman who conducted various business enterprises in London: as dancing master, theatre owner, bookseller, printer and translator.[1] He is remembered chiefly for his *Brittania*, an atlas of 100 road maps of England and Wales, 'printed by the Author at his House in White-Fryers' in 1675. The long sub-title reveals the nature of the work: *an Illustration of the Kingdom of England and Dominion of Wales by a Geographical and Historical Description of the Principal Roads* . . .

*Brittania* is a beautifully produced folio volume with 100 copper engraved plates. Each plate has six or seven 'strips' which show sections of a *Principal Road*, either 'direct' from London or between other 'eminent places'. In several ways the publication 'took a major step forward in the mapping of England'.[2] There had been earlier road maps but Ogilby's were based on original field-work, with distance measured by a wheel dimensurator; the statute mile of 1,760 yards was used for the first time in an atlas; the maps were drawn on a uniform scale of one inch to one mile; and the distances from the beginning of each route were marked on the maps. Not surprisingly Ogilby's work remained the basis of later atlases until the foundation of the Ordnance Survey in 1791; while his distances were used for the location of 18th-century milestones.

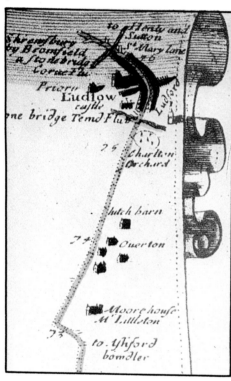

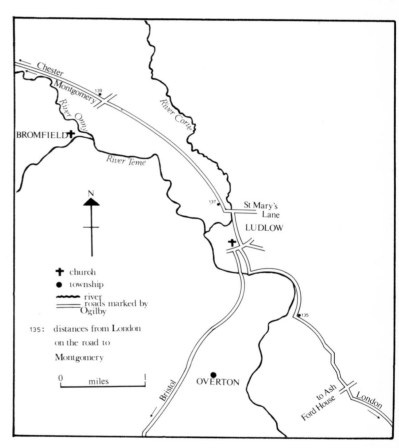

The top of one of Ogilby's scroll-like strips, taken from The Road from Bristol to Chester (plate 56). The church, the castle and the stone bridge over the Teme are marked while 'Priory', though wrongly located, must refer to the remains of the Carmelite Friary in Corve Street. South of the town the details are comparable to those shown on the 1577 map (see p.39) but 'Charlton's orchard' is also shown. This was part of the ancient manor of Ludford, then held by Sir Job Charlton (1614-97), Chief Justice of Chester.

This sketch map, based on a modern O.S. survey, shows the two principal roads which passed through Ludlow: the road from London to Montgomery (Ogilby's plate 44) and the road from Bristol to Chester (plates 56-7). These routes used the same course north west of Ludlow, so in effect the map shows the three major roads which converged on Ludlow at this time. These old routes were largely superseded after 1756 by the new roads of the Ludlow Turnpike Trusts but sections can be traced along narrow lanes and overgrown trackways, e.g. the minor road from Burford which comes to Ludlow over Tinkers' Hill.

1. Chudd,T., *The Printed Maps in the Atlases of Great Britain and Ireland* (1927), p.444.
2. Harley,J.B., introduction to 1970 reprint of *Brittania Depicta or Ogilby Improved* (1720), p.3.

On 14 July 1684 Henry, first Duke of Beaufort and Lord President of Wales, commenced a Progress of inspection of his command which was to last just over five weeks. Among his retinue was Thomas Dineley, a Herefordshire gentleman and seasoned traveller, who had the fortunate habit of writing a detailed account of what he saw together with making careful sketches of views and buildings. It is not clear whether his journal was commissioned or was his own idea but similar accounts survive of Dineley's travels to Flanders, France and Ireland, together with an antiquarian survey of church monuments entitled *History from Marble*. This last work breaks off only a few weeks before the commencement of the account of the Beaufort progress which was to be entitled *Notitia Cambro-Brittanica*.

Ludlow, as the headquarters of the Council in the Marches of Wales, was visited twice during the Progress during which time Dineley had the opportunity to take notes and sketch what he saw. The resulting drawings are the earliest known views of the town to have survived and are remarkable in catching the Castle in its heyday as the Council's headquarters, and only five years before its final dissolution and decay.

Dineley's prospect of Ludlow from Whitcliffe shows a view which in many ways has changed little in 300 years. On the right the town wall can be seen dipping away, with Dinham gate straddling the road. In the foreground lie the Castle mills and the old Dinham bridge with its timber spans built on five stone piers. This had been rebuilt in 1649, possibly after flood damage.

Within the inner ward of the Castle we are shown a view of *Prince Arthur's Chappel* with its famous circular nave which still exists today. Dedicated to St Mary Magdalene, it was probably built during the first quarter of the 12th century and is of what might be regarded as the Templar pattern. It is shown here with the chancel erected during Sir Henry Sidney's time as President (1560-86) replacing the original apsidal Norman structure. A little gabled roof surmounts the nave, shown with its rainwater pipe; and in the foreground, marked A, we see *The Leaden Fountain*, another addition of Sidney's day, the foundations of which were revealed by excavation in 1903-4.

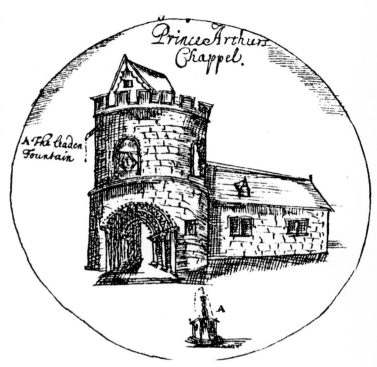

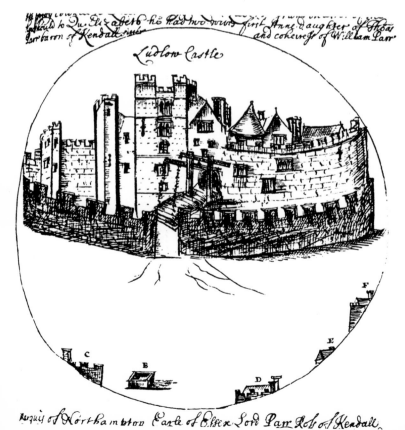

Here Dineley has projected himself into the air to look over the outer wall of the Castle towards the inner ward. In the foreground, marked C, are the coach house and stables (built 1597) with B probably an associated drinking trough. D is the prison and the porter's lodge, built in 1552. The inner buildings are shown in their prime; the roofs are in good repair and we see a drawbridge together with a castellated wall built around the outside of the dry inner ditch.

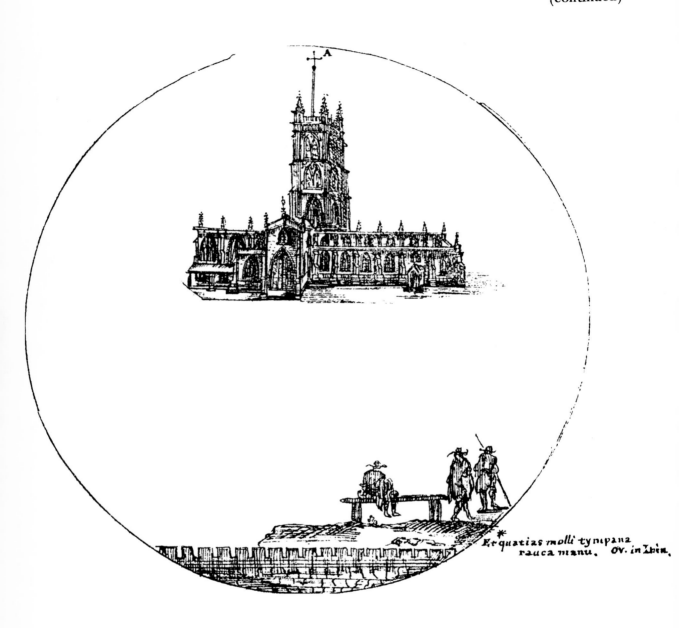

Dineley's view of St Laurence's Parish Church shows it much as it is today, the only addition being a small porch over the door in the north aisle. In the foreground we see the castellated top to the town wall, while the Church weather-vane, marked A, is where 'one of near 60 years of age with a Drum' sat 'beating of a march, which he continued from his Grace entry into the Town untill he came to the Castle'. This illustration has been borrowed from Dineley's earlier manuscript *History from Marble* and it is there that he relates the legend of the iron arrow in the gable of the north transept of Ludlow Church:

*On the outside upon the ridge of the north Cross Isle is seen a long bearded arrow of Iron sticking direct sayd to be sett there in commemoration of a shott made by Robin Hood from the Old Field a long mile distant which hitt the steeple.*

In reality it marks the fletchers' chancel, the chantry chapel of the arrow-makers, and was placed there as their emblem.

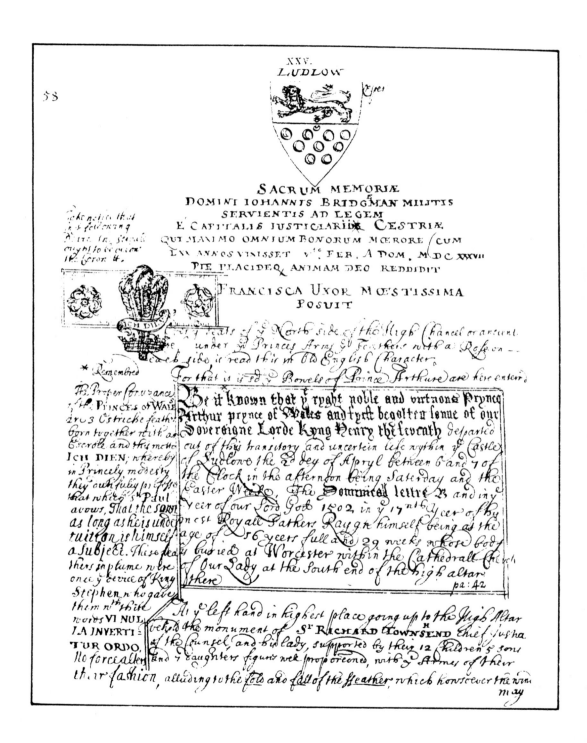

A typical page from the Dineley manuscript. Here he describes the monumental inscriptions in the Parish Church, principally the memorial to the death of Prince Arthur, eldest son of Henry VII, in Ludlow Castle in 1502, 'an account whereof is painted on high in old English Characters in Ludlow'.

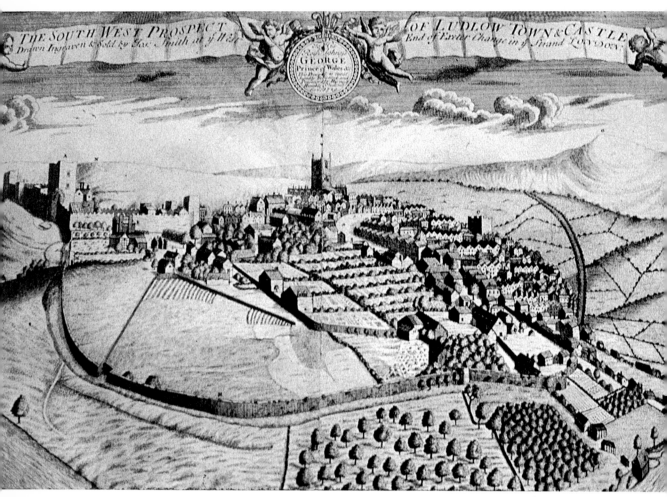

Joseph Smith was an engraver and publisher who operated from 'ye West End of Exeter Change in ye Strand, London'. His large panoramic engraving of Ludlow, made in 1719, is the best known of the 18th century prospects of the town. It was published in 1724 in *Nouveau Theatre de la Grande Bretagne*, a massive work in four volumes, and also in *Brittania Illustrata*, another contemporary work.

The engraving measures 20½ in. by 18 in. At first glance it is quite impressive on account of its size and apparent detail but close examination reveals a confused muddle, particularly at the eastern end of the town, shown on the right hand side of the plate. In the bottom right hand corner Broad Street and Mill Street can easily be identified—Broad Street as the continuation of Ludford Bridge, Mill Street by the Grammar School (marked D)—but their courses appear to merge before sweeping round to the east just below the church. Perhaps this area was sketched from two different positions and the two streets were confused when the final version was drawn, probably when the artist was back in London.

Typically in the style of the day the major buildings are shown relatively larger than the rest of the town. The castle and the church are fairly well drawn, though the nave of the latter has been sketched in from another view-point, as it would be end-on from where the engraving was taken. Galdeford Tower (C), the Grammar School (D) and Dinham House are all shown with what seem to be accurate details. East of the town can be seen Rock Lane, the entrenched boundary between the ancient parishes of Stanton Lacy and Ludford and probably the oldest man-made feature on the picture.

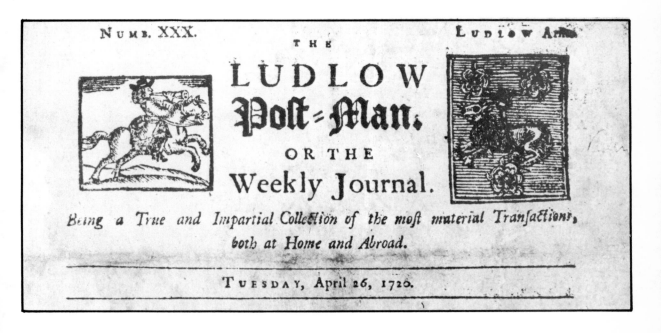

Ludlow's first known newspaper, *The Ludlow Postman*, was published weekly from 9 October 1719 until 26 April 1720, or later.[1] The post-man or post-boy, carrying the mail and other messages on hired horses from one post inn to the next, was a familiar contemporary figure. The newspaper heading, reproduced above, shows a mounted post-man with his horn and also a rather crude version of the Ludlow arms (see p. 99).

The editor and publisher was a young printer, William Parks (c.1695-1750), who had been apprenticed to Stephen Bryan of Worcester, founder of *The Worcester Postman*.[2] He was in Ludlow between 1718 and 1721, occupying what is now No. 4 Bull Ring with his wife, journeyman and maid.[3] By March 1725/26 he was in North America, becoming a highly esteemed printer in Virginia, where over 150 publications bear his imprint.[4] *A Collection of all the Acts of Assembly*, published at Williamsburg in 1732, has a list of some 300 subscribers, several of whom came from south Shropshire, including Mr. Richard Parks, Ludlow's town clerk.

Much of *The Ludlow Postman* was copied from other publications but this kind of 'scissors and paste' journalism was quite normal. Parks did include items of local interest and some of these seek to attract readers by sensation and gossip, the technique of *Private Eye*. Such an item in the first issue concerns David Valentine (d.1766), who became landlord of the *Bear* and was later organist at the parish church.[5] The *Bear Inn* was at No. 45 Bull Ring (now Boots chemists), across the street from Parks' shop; and perhaps had the constellation as its sign, hence the play on the word 'Plough'. The extract gives a rare glimpse of an early 18th century wedding:

*Ludlow, October 8. Tuesday last being Valentines Day (or the day that Mr. Valentine Musician put his hand to the Plough, in order for Seedness . . .) was celebrated a marriage between the said Mr. Valentine and one Mrs. Downes of the Plough Inn in this Town; and with more Uncommon Splendour than hath been known by any of this Place, for going to church Mrs. Bride was led up guarded by two Officers, and Mr. Bridegroom came next, attended by two ladies of the best Quality about this place, and after there followed a numerous Train of Gentlemen and Ladies in Couples, a Dragoon and his Spouse concluding the Rear. After the Nuptial Ceremonies were performed, the Company was entertained with a very handsome Dinner, and the whole Day was attended with Ringing of Bells, Musick and Dancing, which they prolonged (to the great Uneasiness of Mr. Bridegroom) till 3 o'clock the next Morning; at which Time they concluded the Solemnity with Sock-Possets and the usual Custom of Throwing the Stocking; and I hear many Persons have stood less pelted in the Pillory than they were on the Bed . . .*

1. Eleven copies are in the B.L., including no.1. No.30 is in private ownership.
2. We are indebted to Mr. Rockwell Smith of Virginia for this and other information on Parks.
3. Easter Books 1718-21; window tax assessment 1721.
4. Wroth, L.C., *William Parks: Printer and Journalist of England and Colonial America* (1926), p.11
5. *L.P.R.*, p.719: married, 6 October 1719, David Valentine and Anne Downes, both of this parish; Francis, R., and Klein, P., *The Organs and Organists of Ludlow Parish Church*, p.37

William Stukeley (1687-1765) was a doctor, an antiquarian and a clergyman, and one of the great intellectual all-rounders of the 18th century.[1] After education in Lincolnshire and Cambridge he became a successful London doctor and a Fellow of the College of Physicians. He was a close friend of Sir Isaac Newton and in 1717, when only just 30, was elected a Fellow of the Royal Society. In 1718 he was a founder member and secretary of the Society of Antiquaries and went on long antiquarian tours, partly to alleviate his gout! He was ordained in 1729 and was first Vicar of Stamford, then of a fashionable London church. Many stories survive of these incumbencies, e.g. that he postponed a service so that the congregation could watch an eclipse.

He came to Ludlow in September 1721 and included a description and drawings of the town in his *Itinerarium Curiosum: an Account of the Antiquities and remarkable Curiositys in Nature, observed in travels through Great Britain*, which was published in 1724. He had an eye for the unusual and his account includes details not mentioned by other writers.

Stukeley begins with a description of the site of Ludlow and of the weirs on the River Teme:

*'Our next expedition was to Ludlow, a place of fame and antiquity . . . this town is wall'd quite round and pretty strong . . . scituate upon a hill top . . . on which, precipitous to the north and west, stands the castle. On the south side runs the Teme, fetter'd with numerous dams across, in nature of cataracts, by which means abundance of mills are turn'd. The superfluous water pours over 'em cascade like, with a mighty noise.'*

His description of the Parish Church includes an interesting reference to the small room in the east wall of the chancel, which puzzled Cranage and other church historians.[2]

*(Above) The 13th-century window which Stukeley described as 'strongly barr'd'. It was moved to its present position in the 15th century.*

*'Here is a very good church and handsome tower with a pleasant ring of six bells in the cross thereof. the windows are full of painted glass pretty entire. there are some old monuments of the lords presidents, etc., and an inscription upon the north wall of the quire relating to prince Arthur, who dyed here. his bowels were bury'd in this place. one told me they took up his heart not long since in a leaden box. in the eastern angle of the quire is a closet, antiently call'd the God-house, where the priests lock'd up their roods, wafers, and such things. it has a window strongly barr'd outward.[3] This church is consecrate to St Laurence . . .'*

The next sentence is the only description we have of the ancient High Cross which stood south west of the present Butter Cross, in front of the building now known as Tamberlaine House.[4] Documents show that the Cross was a covered building with open sides, though part was enclosed as a 'little room'. It was demolished in 1744 when the conduit was removed to a site in Church Street, where it remained until c.1900.

*'. . . in the mercat-place is an exagonal cistern or conduit like a cross, on the top of which is a long stone cross bearing a nich with an image of that saint (St Laurence) in it.'*

*The Cross at Chichester which the High Cross at Ludlow resembled. The Ludlow Cross was built in the 15th century, replacing a simpler structure.*

1. *D.N.B.*
2. Cranage, pp. 113-115.
3. Cranage concludes that the closet was probably a sacristy, where the Sanctus bell was rung at the elevation of the Host.
4. Weyman, 1913, pp. 10-13.

*This fragment of a manorial map of Bromfield, made for the Herberts in 1733, shows a property on the right (now the entrance to the yard of Lloyds of Ludlow Ltd., Transport Contractors) which was part of their estate. On the left, in Linney turn, is a thumbnail sketch of St Leonard's chapel, included to identify the locality. This is the only picture of the chapel yet found, for it was demolished by the Corporation some 50 years later. The western tower with small spire can be clearly seen.*

Stukeley goes on to describe the college of the Palmers' Guild, then owned by Thomas Meyricke (d. 1724), mercer and wool stapler.[5] The reference to a painting by Hans Holbein (1497-1543) supports the evidence of probate inventories that some Ludlovians owned the work of well known artists.[6]

*'west of the church was a college, now converted to a dwelling house, whose owner showed us a pretty collection of pictures, one by Holbein.'*

Stukeley's comments on the lower part of Corve Street suggest that some fragments of the Carmelite Friary remained above ground, though he repeats the popular error that St Leonard's chapel once belonged to it. The 'arched gateway' was 'the lower barre of Corve', first built in the 13th century though rebuilt after the 17th century Civil War.

*'There was a rich priory out of the town on the north side, small ruins now to be seen, except a little adjoyning church once belonging to it. about the same place an arched gate-way went cross the street, but now demolished.'*

*The inner courtyard of the College in 1878, before it was converted to a hospital. The pedimented central block was added to the medieval buildings in 1715, a few years before Stukeley's visit.*

5. PRO: Prob. 11, 601. The Meyrickes were a trading family from London and Southampton who later built Dinham Lodge, where they lived until the early 20th century.
6. e.g. of Sarah Purefoy (PRO: Prob. 5/4921).

Stukeley concludes with a detailed account of the ruined castle:

*the greatest rarity of Ludlow is the noble and strong castle and palace, plac'd on the north-west angle of the town upon a rock, commanding a delightful prospect north-ward, but on the west where runs the river 'tis over-looked by a high hill. 'Tis strongly environ'd by embattailed walls of great height and thickness, with towers at convenient distances. that half which is within the walls of the town is secur'd moreover with a deep ditch. the other founded on the solid rock. It's divided into two separate parts: the castle properly so speaking, wherein the palace and lodgings; and the green or out-work . . . the first is in the strongest or north-west corner, and has likewise walls and ditch hewn out of the rock towards the green. this was the residence of the lords presidents, 'twas a nobl structure, but now alas only groans out with its last breath the glorys of its antient state. A chappel here has abundance of coats of arms upon the pannels, so has the hall, together with lances, spears, firelocks and old armour; but the present inhabitants live upon the sale of the timber, stone, iron, and other materials and furniture, which dwindle away insensibly. here dy'd prince Arthur. The green takes in a large compass of ground wherein was formerly the court of judicature and records, the stables, garden, bowling green and other offices, all which now lye in ruins, or are let out at rack-rents to those that pilfer what they can. over several of the stable doors are Q.Elizabeth's arms, the earls of Pembroke's and others.*

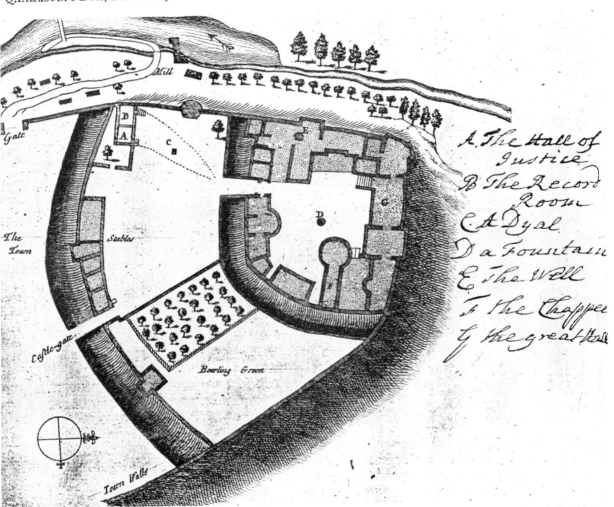

A. The Hall of Justice
B The Record Room
C A Dyal
D a Fountain
E The Well
F The Chappel
G the great Hall

*In shape and detail this plan is much inferior to that made by T.F.Pritchard some 50 years later but it is of interest as the oldest extant plan of the Castle. It shows the extent of the built up area within the inner bailey.*

## 1722

Daniel Defoe (c.1661-1731) was a prolific journalist and pamphleteer, though today his best known work is the novel *Robinson Crusoe* (1719). He was brought up a Dissenter and had an eventful adult life, going bankrupt as a young businessman and later being prosecuted and pilloried for libelling the Church of England.

Defoe's *Tour through Great Britain* was first published in instalments between 1724 and 1726 but his visit to Ludlow was made in 1722, a year after that made by Stukeley. Defoe's interests were political rather than antiquarian and this is reflected in his comments. He probably exaggerates the effect of the abolition of the Council of the Marches on the town's economy.

> The Castle of Ludlow shows in its Decay, what it was in its flourishing Estate: It is the Palace of the Princes of Wales, that is, to speak more properly, it is annexed to the Principality of Wales; which is the Appanage of the Heir Apparent, and this is his Palace in right of his being made Prince of Wales.
>
> The situation of this Castle is most Beautiful indeed . . . The Country round it is exceeding pleasant, fertile, populous, and the Soil rich; nothing can be added by Nature to make it a Place fit for a Royal Palace: It wants only the Residence of its Princes, but that is not now to be expected.
>
> The Castle itself is in the very Perfection of Decay, all the fine Courts, the Royal Appartments, Halls, and Rooms of State, lye open, abandoned and some of them falling down; for since the Courts of the President and Marches are taken away, here is nothing to do that requires the Attendance of any publick People; so that time, the great Devourer of the Works of Men, begins to eat into the very Stone Walls, and to spread the Face of Royal Ruins upon the whole Fabrick.
>
> The Town of Ludlow is a tolerable Place, but it decays to be sure with the rest . . . 'tis on the Bank of the Teme, over which it has a good Bridge, and it was formerly a Town of good Trade.
>
> King Henry VIII Established the Court of the President here, and the Council of the Marches, and all Causes of 'nisi prius', or of Civil Rights were try'd here . . . but this Court was entirely taken away by Act of Parliament in our Days, and this, as above, tends to the sensible Decay of the Town as well as of the Castle.

*This early aerial photograph was perhaps taken by the Royal Flying Corps during the 1914-18 war. It shows the 'Beautiful indeed' situation of the Castle as noted by Defoe, as well as the ruined buildings themselves. The photograph illustrates other points of interest to the urban historian, especially the rectilinear field pattern in Linney, to the left of the Castle (see p.120). The line of the original High Street, running east from the Castle, can also be clearly seen. At the top of the picture are the slopes between Gravel Hill and Corve Street, where there were teynters' yards in the late Middle Ages.*

1. *D.N.B.*

*A panoramic view of Ludlow facing north east.*

This fine panoramic view of Ludlow, painted in 1722, was the result of co-operation between two artists: Isaac Vogelsanck (1688-1753) and Bernard Lens (1682-1740). Vogelsanck was an immigrant from Holland who had studied in Amsterdam under Huchtenberg, one of the last of the great Dutch school of painters of the 17th century.[1] He arrived in London about 1715 and was best known for his painted ceilings. Lens became eminent as Court Miniaturist to George II and as drawing master to the Duke of Cumberland, perhaps being best known for his miniature copies of old masters such as Van Dyck.[2]

The painting was commissioned by Richard Salwey (1675-1760) of the Moor, Richard's Castle, just two miles south of Ludlow. The Salweys can be seen in the foreground. The Salweys have been closely involved in Ludlow affairs from the 17th century to the present day. Richard himself was elected to the Corporation in 1712 and for much of the century Nos. 17, 18 and 52 Broad Street were leased or owned by the family as town houses. It was quite common for topographical and other paintings to be commissioned from London artists in this way.

1. Strickland,W.G., *A Dictionary of Irish Artists*, vol.2 (1913), p.491
2. *D.N.B.*

The painting, measuring 60 by 36 in., is remarkable for its painstaking attention to detail. It is noticeable that the River Teme in the foreground seems to bulge out towards the observer as if seen through a fish-eye camera lens. This is strongly indicative that the initial drawings for the picture were prepared with the aid of a camera obscura, a device widely used at this time to give an accuracy otherwise impossible before the advent of photography. If this is so the panorama is virtually as good as a photograph and is a remarkable document indeed.

In 1722 Ludlow had a population just under 2,000. The picture is taken from Whitcliffe, the town's common land since the Middle Ages. It shows the great sweep of the River Teme, with the castle strategically sited above the steepest slopes. Dinham Bridge can be seen on the far left and Ludford Bridge on the far right, with Titterstone Clee Hill on the skyline. The town wall was still intact along its whole length, except for a few breaches near Dinham. In the north, east and south important built up areas were outside the town wall but the picture shows that much of the western part of Ludlow was still undeveloped, both inside and outside the walls.

*The town centre, Camp Lane and Christ Croft.*
The tower of the Parish Church dominates the centre of the town while Galdeford Tower can be seen further east. The crescent-shaped piece of land inside the town wall was burgaged in the 15th century but later became 'a close with two barns', leased by the Corporation for 13s. p.a. Beyond, Camp Lane is more rural and has a more sinuous shape than the surfaced road of today. The most interesting feature is the trackway at right angles to the town wall, leading down to the river. This is a remnant of Christ Croft, originally a defensive ditch east of Dinham but later incorporated into the gridiron town plan as a rear access lane. Christ Croft was truncated when the town walls were built in the late 13th century but its course can be followed through the gate into Camp Lane and then between the houses fronting to Dinham and Mill Street, though perspective distorts its straight line.

*The southern part of the town.*
On the extreme left is a semi-circular bastion, one of the few surviving defensive works on the town wall. In the foreground is part of the Lord's Orchard, so called because in the Middle Ages it was in the demesne of the manorial lord; in 1722 it was held by Richard Salwey, the patron of this panorama, at £1 p.a. as a lessee of the Corporation. Beyond can be seen the southern suburbs of Ludlow, between the wall and the River Teme. This area had been burgaged in the Middle Ages and was an important cloth-making district but many of the houses were burnt in the Civil War of 1642-6. By 1722 most of Lower Broad Street and parts of Holdgate Fee had been rebuilt but Lower Mill Street was still sparsely developed. The curious chimney-like feature between Mill Gate and the river has yet to be identified.

*Mill Gate, Broad Gate and Rock Lane.*
This detail gives what is probably the only accurate likeness of Mill Gate: a small cylindrical tower with a conical roof in which was probably only a small postern gate. The gate was demolished by the Corporation only three years after the picture was made to improve access to the river and the mill. Beyond, can be seen the substantial house over the more important Broad Gate; this is the only known picture of the Broad Gate before it was extended some 30 years later when Dr. Sprott was lessee. Buildings which were later incorporated into the house called Merivale can be seen just inside Mill Gate. Stretching towards Broad Gate is a range of four buildings, the second of which is Barnaby House, a medieval stone mansion which once belonged to Thomas Barnaby, Cofferer to Edward IV; the stone walls of the large garden can be clearly seen. Some distance left of the Broad Gate is a very large house with five visible gables; this is probably 'the Fayre House', built by Edmund Walter c.1570 and in 1722 the town house of the Lloyds of Maesyfylin in Cardiganshire (remnants of this house are preserved in Nos. 35-37 Broad Street). In the far distance, rising almost vertically across the landscape, is Rock Lane, the entrenched parish boundary between Ludford and Stanton Lacy.

*Central Dinham on the 1:500 O.S. map of 1885 (right).*

*The south west corner of the Castle and adjoining parts of Dinham (above).*
The Castle walls were still well preserved while the intact roofs of the Judges Chambers, built in the late 16th century, can be seen east of the Norman keep. The recreational walks round the Castle were not laid out until 1772 so the picture shows the wall of the outer bailey still unpierced by the arched opening through which one of these walks was taken. Below the Castle Dinham Gate can be seen edge on, with castellated parapets. In the foreground the line of the extra-mural ditch can just be distinguished. Next to the Castle wall is Dinham House, built in 1716 and soon after bought by Richard Knight, the rich iron master from Downton. One of the wings added in 1748 engulfed the external chimney stacks. The picture also gives a unique glimpse of the property just to the south of Dinham House, which was demolished later in the century when the present Dinham Lodge was built. In the 17th century this was leased by the Corporation to members of the Bowdler family, Ludlow's leading mercers.

*Dinham and the outer gate of the Castle (below).*
There was probably a small civilian settlement at Dinham some years before the new town of Ludlow was developed further east during the 12th century. The unroofed shell of St Thomas's chapel can be seen. It was founded in the late 12th century, reroofed by the Corporation in 1557 but had become a ruin by the 18th century. The chapel is on a wedge-shaped piece of land, parts of which were described as a graveyard as late as the 17th century. By the 18th century houses had been built south of the chapel though the triangular piece of land to the north was still open, as it is today. The picture shows houses lining the narrow street east of the chapel, including the long range with four dormers, the rear wall of which is now part of No. 16 Dinham. The picture gives a unique view of the cluster of buildings round the outer gate of the Castle, most of which had their roofs intact.

Edward Lloyd (c.1668-c.1730) was the son of Marmaduke Lloyd of Drenewydd in the parish of Whittington in the north-west of Shropshire. He matriculated at Oxford in 1683 and was later called to the bar at the Inner Temple in London.[1] It is reported that 'during the early part of his life in the metropolis . . . he employed his leisure hours in translating from the public records whatever might in any way relate to or illustrate the history of his native county . . .'[2] Before the Public Record Office was opened in 1838 many state papers were housed in the Temple and others in nearby Chancery Lane but though access was easy Lloyd would have lacked the careful cataloguing and other aids available to the modern scholar.[3] When he 'retired to his patrimonial seat . . . he digested a part of his extensive collections which he entitled *Antiquities of Shropshire.'*

Two sections of the Ludlow part of Lloyd's manuscript, which is in the Local Studies Library at Shrewsbury, are reproduced below. One relates to the Palmers' Guild, founded in the mid-13th century, and the other to the Carmelite Friary, founded in 1350. In both cases the text is a digest of information gathered from different original documents and Lloyd anticipates the methods of modern historical scholarship by giving his references in adjoining notes. To some extent Camden used this technique in the late 16th century but he was working from narrative chronicles, not from State papers like the Patent Rolls. Though the notation system is now different, most of Lloyd's references have been picked up by modern scholars, e.g. in the articles by Alec Gaydon in the second volume of the *Victoria County History of Shropshire* (1973). No earlier examples of this work have been found and Lloyd must stand unchallenged as Ludlow's first documentary historian.

1. Foster; this Edward Lloyd is not to be confused with Edward Lhuyd, the Shropshire botanist, geologist, archaeologist and philologist (1660-1709), whose life is described by P.W. Carter in *Shropshire Conservation Trust Bulletin*, no.9, March 1967.
2. This and other quotations are from Jukes.
3. *Guide to the Contents of the Public Record Office* (1963), pp.1, 7.

The only known copy of Lloyd's manuscript passed into the hands of the Rev. William Mytton (1711-46) of Halston, only a few miles away from Drenewydd in the north of Shropshire. The Myttons are commonly thought of as a family of hard-riding, heavy-drinking country squires, personified by the eccentric 'mad Jack' Mytton (1796-1834); but William was a serious-minded clergyman, who became Rector of Habberley, south-west of Shrewsbury, and is remembered as 'an antiquary and a Shropshire genealogist'.[1]

It is likely that Mytton 'made additions' to the Lloyd manuscript but he also did considerable work in his own right towards a County history. Several large volumes of 'Mytton Papers' are deposited in Birmingham University Library, one of which is devoted almost entirely to Ludlow. This contains a few sheets of manuscript notes and over 100 drawings, a few of them beautifully coloured. These are all of memorials in the Parish Church or of coats of arms in the Castle, many of which no longer survive. The two reproduced below are representative samples of Mytton's work and illustrate his careful drawing as well as his interest in heraldry and genealogy. Both relate to the Council of the Marches, which had its headquarters at Ludlow Castle.

*These six coats of arms, carefully copied by Mytton, were part of a series of oak panels inside the chapel of St Mary Magdalene in the Castle. Sometime between 1768 and 1794 they were removed to the Bull Hotel, where they remained until the early years of the 20th century, when they mysteriously disappeared.[2] The lowest pair of arms belonged to eminent Elizabethans: Henry Herbert, Earl of Pembroke (1534-1601), who was Lord President from 1586; and Sir John Puckering (1544-96), who held many legal posts as well as being Justice of Carmarthen. Both these arms were erected in 1586, when Pembroke took office. Above are four coats of arms erected in November 1616 as part of the local celebrations when Charles Stuart became Prince of Wales. One is of Lord Gerard, who was only Lord President for a very short period; the others, all earls, were ordinary members of the Council.*

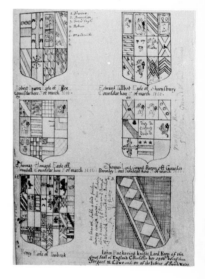

*A pencil note, written upside down below the drawing, says that this fine memorial to Dame Mary Eure, wife of Lord Eure, was 'against ye South wall of ye high Chancell of Ludlow Church' when Mytton drew it in 1734. The tilt of the monument is due to the way in which the paper has been fastened in the bound volume, rather than to careless technique. Although the decoration is less lavish, this tomb has similarities to that of the Walters (see p.38). The effigy is on its side to save floor space. She wears late Elizabethan costume, which is beautifully carved. Lord Eure himself died just over four years later but he had already resigned the Presidency to Lord Gerard, thus the entry 'late Ld. President' against his name in the parish register. He was the only holder of the office to be buried at Ludlow but no memorial was erected.*

1. Holdsworth, J., *Mango: The Life and Times of Squire John Mytton* (1972); Foster.
2. Wright (1852), p.454; Baker, p.18.

*This painting gives a glimpse of Broad Street when its 18th-century 'modernisation' was nearly complete. In 1766 the most recent change had been at No. 27, refronted two years before by T. F. Pritchard of Shrewsbury. The next change occurred two years later when the* Seven Stars *at No. 38 was replaced by the five-bay Georgian mansion which still occupies the site.*

Samuel Scott (*c.*1710-72) was an important topographical artist who was described by a near contemporary as 'the first painter of his own age'.[1] He painted buildings with 'consumate skill' and has been called 'the English Canaletto'.

For most of his life he lived in London but in 1765 he moved to Ludlow to be near his daughter, who had married a local schoolmaster. For three years he was a tenant of what is now No. 35 Broad Street, but he then moved to Bath, in the hope that the waters would ease the gout which 'harassed and tormented him most of his life'.[2]

His best known Ludlow painting is that of Broad Street, probably painted in 1766.

The residents of these houses can be identified from window tax returns and other sources.[3] As shown below, the lower part of the street had a considerable social mix, with the richer citizens generally occupying the larger houses.

As was his common practice Scott introduces some of the residents into his picture. The portly gentleman on the steps of No. 27 is almost certainly Somerset Davies, a successful mercer who had been Bailiff three times. The stooping figure with the dog in front of No. 36 is probably the attorney, Mr. Toldervy, while further up the street, in front of the Seven Stars, are John Thomas and his wife, holding the youngest of their seven children. Scott has contrived a window on the far right of the picture so that Alexander Stuart of No. 33 can be included; while the demure young lady next door is probably Miss Harriett Price, daughter of Mrs. Price, widow. Stuart and Miss Price were certainly good neighbours—and perhaps a little more—for when he made his will in 1782 he left £100 to Miss Harriett Price 'as a grateful acknowledgement of her long invaluable friendship and friendly attendance on me during my long confinement'.[4]

1. Pilkington, Rev. M., *A Dictionary of Painters* (1805), p. 380.
2. *D.N.B.*; Bryan, vol. 5, p. 58.
3. The method is described in Speight and Lloyd; more detail on these houses is available in Lloyd (1979).
4. P.R.O: Prob. 11/1140 fo. 184.

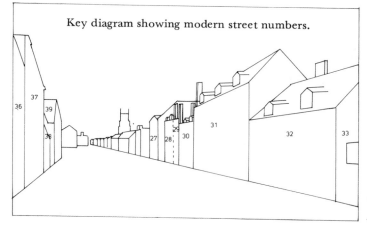

Key diagram showing modern street numbers.

The enlargement below of a small part of Scott's painting gives a picture of the eastern side of the street above Brand Lane. On the right, with a prominent sign board, is the Peacock Inn (No. 22), kept by William Haycock, and next to it, with the gable end to the street, is the house of Mrs. Fewtrell, widow (21/20). The next two houses (19 & 18), very little changed today, were Corporation properties, rebuilt in 1737 and 1738 respectively and leased to Herbert Cole, surgeon, and Mrs. Salwey of Richard's Castle. To the left the five-bay house with dormer windows (17), which had been built to contract in 1704, was also leased to the Salweys but was occupied by a relative, Mrs. Ward. The largest house (16), with the long, high roof, belonged to the influential Baugh family and was occupied by Mrs. Walcott from Bitterley. This house, regrettably, was replaced by Lloyd's Bank in 1879. On the far left is the house of Samuel Waring (15), one of the town's master glovers.

| Modern house number | Name in window tax assessment, 1766 | status/occupation | From Easter Rate book, 1766 other adults/servants | assessment |
|---|---|---|---|---|
| 23 | Miss Sprott | | sister and maid | 7s 6d |
| 24/5 | William Debitett | smith | wife | 1s 6d |
| 26 | Mrs. Bradshaw | widow | son, daughter & maid | 2s 6d |
| 27 | Somerset Davies Esq | (mercer) | wife, 3 men, 2 maids | £1 1s 0d |
| 28 | Robert Jones Esq. | | wife & maid | 10s 6d |
| 29 | Mr. Thomas Jones (+ Joseph Harris | organist) | wife & maid | 5s 0d |
| 30 | Robert Pitt (+ John Toldervy | plumber innkeeper) | wife | 1s 4d |
| 31 | John Aingell | currier | wife & maid | 5s 0d |
| 32 | Mrs. Price | widow | daughter & maid | 5s 0d |
| 33 | Alexander Stuart | (not resident: spent part of each year in Scotland) | | |
| 35 | Mr. Scott | (house not on picture) | wife & maid | 10s 6d |
| 36 | Mr. Toldervy | attorney | wife, clerk, man & maid | 10s 6d |
| 37 | Rev. Mr. Poole | | wife, 2 daughters, 2 maids | 10s 6d |
| 38 | John Thomas | innkeeper (The Seven Stars) | wife | 1s 4d |
| 39 | Mrs. Ashwood | widow | daughter, man & 2 maids | £1 1s 0d |

After the dissolution of the Council of the Marches in 1689 Ludlow Castle remained Crown property but no effective use was made of it. Governors were appointed, the last of them Alexander Stuart of Fife (d.1786; see pp.68-9), a relative of the royal Stuarts;[1] but the office was a sinecure and in 1765 Francis Grose tellingly referred to Stuart as 'a sort of Governor'.[2] A series of travel writers, including Stukeley and Defoe (see p.61), refer to the progressive despoliation while in the 1740s Pennie Marsh, son of a local writing-master, wrote that 'the brave old castle' had 'quite gone to decay'.[3]

The drawings below are two of a series drawn in 1765, probably by order of the Earl of Powis.[4] They are the best visual record we have of the appearance of the Castle at this time. Henry Arthur Herbert (d.1772), made Earl of Powis by the second creation in 1748, had been a member of Ludlow Corporation since 1729 and was a generous benefactor to the town, e.g. in 1764 a handsome Snetzler organ was installed in the Parish Church at his expense. These drawings are the first evidence of his interest in the Castle, which he took on a long lease in 1771 and which his grandson bought in 1811.

View of Keep and Governor's House from Outer Court. *The keep is shown in rather better condition than it is today but the greatest interest attaches to the buildings on the right. These were erected in 1581 by Sir Henry Sidney, whose arms are in the niche over the older arched entrance. In 1765 these buildings still had a partially intact roof, probably because they were tiled and therefore less affected than other parts of the Castle by the order issued c.1715 to strip the roofs of their lead, presumably to use it for other purposes. The buildings are generally referred to as the Judges Lodgings but they may have served as a Governor's House for some of the post-1689 period.*

View of Keep and Governor's House from Inner Court. *This side of the roof of the Governor's House has lost more of its tiles but the hexagonal newel staircase still has its conical roof intact. The Keep was swathed in ivy, an essential ingredient in the Castle's metamorphosis into a picturesque ruin; for here, in the words of a eulogy 'written at midnight amongst the ruins of Ludlow Castle:* . . . the bat and moping owl are found,
And mould'ring turrets intercept the way . . .'[5]

1. Hodges,W., *An Historical Account of Ludlow Castle* (1794), pp.44-5.
2. Grose, F., *The Antiquities of England and Wales*: Shropshire (1765), p. 14.
3. Manuscript notebook of the late Mr. W. Nash of Ludlow.
4. Copies in Ludlow Museum.
5. Hodges, op. cit., p.24.

T.F. Pritchard (1723-75) was a Shrewsbury builder and architect, whose work along the Welsh border has been fully appreciated only in recent years. He built or rebuilt several important buildings in Ludlow and in 1771 was employed by the Government to value the materials at the Castle with a view to its demolition. Thomas Wright (see p.99), writing about this in 1868 but drawing on the memory of his father, who had come to Ludlow in the 1790s, attributed the preservation of the Castle to a subterfuge by Pritchard:

> It is evident that Mr. Pritchard sought to save the building by wonderfully undervaluing the materials, so as to show that they would not pay for the work of destruction; and we have to thank him partly, without doubt, for the prevention of so extraordinary an act of Vandalism.[1]

Pritchard's report was certainly instrumental in persuading the Government that it would be more economical to lease the Castle to the Earl of Powis than to demolish it. The Earl took the lease late in 1771 but he was dead within the year and it was left to his Countess, Barbara, to lay out the recreational walks round the outside of the Castle. There could be no better memorial to this aristocratic act of salvage.

The plan is informative in itself but the report gives further details on the numbered buildings. Extracts from this are reproduced below. The theme of the report is struck in the preamble when Pritchard writes:

> The wall, though in many places very thick, being composed of common stones, used the same as they were got out of the rock, without hewing, are very unsound, and where there are no quoins or coping of red hewn stones to support and bind them together, are in a very bad condition . . .
>
> 1.  The entrance of the castle at a tower extremely ruinous . . . The upper parts daily trickling down and scarce can the old gates be made fast to inclose the castle.
> 7.  Mortimer's Tower, formerly entirely round, the back part since has been repaired with a cross wall, without floor or roof. Walling in a ruinous condition.
> 8.  The gateway into the citadel, and formerly the Judges' apartments to the right. The roofing and floors . . . are almost all fallen in and rotted. What remains hangs impending in a frightful and dangerous manner. The walls except the gateway tower, doors and windows, all composed of rubble work.
> 14. Is the principal part of the body of the castle, formerly containing the hall, council chamber, and other apartments, now in so ruined a condition that 'tis dangerous to go under the walls, and the small part of the roof that remains is hanging and just supported by a few braces.
> 16. Hill the tenant's house, to whom belongs the bowling green, stable, outer court, tennis court, gardens, faggot places, etc. The house, as described by the plan, is a very indifferent building, framed many years since of the old materials of the castle. The roof and slating, being kept in repair by the tenant, is in a bad condition.

He concludes: Were whole premises ordered to be converted into one mount of land or gardens, the stone walling would be of little more value than the expense of taking down, clearing and carrying away rubbish, levelling and making good the land . . .

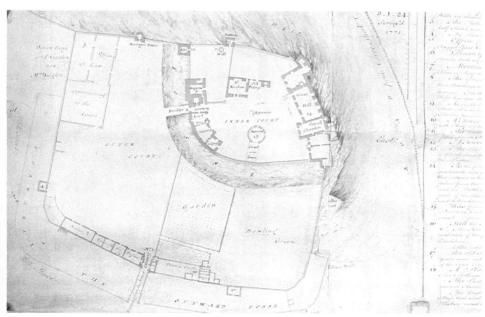

*The plan drawn by Pritchard in 1771.*[2]

1.  Thomas Wright, 'Ludlow Castle', *Archaeologia Cambrensis*, vol. 14, 1868, pp. 142-6.
2.  P.R.O., Maps and plans 2967.

Landscape or topographical painting was very popular in the second half of the 18th century and 'picturesque' subjects were often chosen. It is not surprising that Ludlow Castle was painted many times and by most of the well known topographical artists of the day. Invariably, they viewed the Castle from the western side, so that the River Teme and the steep slopes beyond could be included, but the positions chosen ranged from south west, i.e. on or above the present Bread Walk, round to the north west between Halton Lane and the river. All four paintings chosen here were made after 1772, when formal walks were laid out round the Castle after the Earl of Powis had leased it from the Crown.

The print above, *Part of the Town and Castle of Ludlow*, is based on a view from the north west.[1] It was published in 1775 from a painting by Paul Sandby (1725-1809), a native of Nottingham. Sandby painted 'well-nigh everywhere in Britain' and 'his clear, accurate and decorative manner' was 'the archetype of British view painting'.[2] The tall elms, a favourite device of landscape painters, give a frame to the composition; while the haymakers in the foreground, cheerful and well fed, make it a summer idyll.

*Ludlow Castle, Mill and Weir*, (above), from the south west, was painted by William Marlowe (1740-1813), a protégé and pupil of Samuel Scott (see pp.68-9). Marlowe has been judged 'one of the best landscapists of the 18th century' and 'a particular master of mellow colour'.[3] This painting is a beautiful composition of dark greens and light browns, set against a pale sky. In a manner later perfected by Constable, animals and human figures are introduced into the landscape, some suggesting placidity, others movement and vitality.

1. B.L., K36/15e.        2. Grant, p.169.        3. Ibid, p.123.

*The Perspective View of Ludlow Castle* (above) is one of several Ludlow views that appeared in magazines of the late 18th and early 19th centuries, in this case *The European Magazine* in 1786, and was drawn and engraved by Ravenhill. It is particularly closely observed and shows the recently planted Castle Walk, with the Castle mills, and the ramp leading up to New Bridge on the extreme right. Dinham Gate, demolished in this year, still straddles the road leading into the town. The point from which the view was taken is at the top of Whitcliffe Quarry where the slope to the river falls away dramatically; the foreground therefore with its framing tree, foliage, and 'decayed countrymen' is an artistic device to add interest to the composition.

The picture of *Ludlow Castle* (above) is by J.M.W. Turner (1775-1851), one of the best known of British painters. He came to Ludlow as a young man in 1798 whilst on one of his long walking tours and made sketches of the Castle from at least two positions. Many years later he used one of these sketches, taken from the north west, as a basis for this fine watercolour, one of a series of 103 topographical views painted by Turner and published between 1825 and 1838 by the engraver Charles Heath as *Picturesque Views of England and Wales*.[4] The painting is in the Romantic tradition and though the details of the Castle itself are clearly shown Turner used considerable licence with the surrounding foliage and scenery. The tree on the right, for example, 'is too Italian for Shropshire' though 'it adds to the picture's lyricism', while the harvesters 'share with nature a ripeness that contrasts with the decayed Castle'.[5]

4. Shanes,E., *Turner's Picturesque Views in England and Wales* (1983), pp.10-15.          5. Ibid, p.34.

*A print of* The Angel *c. 1790. Benjamin Fieldhouse became landlord in 1787, three years after John Byng's visit.*

The Hon. John Byng (1742-1813) belonged to a well known naval family but he was commissioned in the army and later worked for the Inland Revenue.[1] Like many rich people of his day he travelled widely for pleasure and the diaries which he kept are exceptional for their 'freshness and freedom from mannerisms'. They were published in 1934 as *The Torrington Diaries*, so called because John Byng became the fifth Viscount Torrington during the last fortnight of his life.

Byng came to Ludlow on 30 June 1784, at an early stage of a 630 mile tour to North Wales. He ignored the economy of Ludlow and the broad base of its social pyramid but his comments give a delightful glimpse of the pleasures and lifestyle of the upper and middle classes during its years as a fashionable social centre.

He and his companions entered the town from the south and his diary account begins with a general appreciation:

*The approach to Ludlow . . . is in the first stile; the river so rapid and translucid, and the view of the town . . . so gratifying. After teaing at our inn (Angel; very good) we walked about the town, admir'd the wideness, and well-building of the streets; and the charming walks around the old castle, overhanging the river banks.*

He continues with a description of the theatre which was on the western side of Mill Street opposite the Grammar School:[2]

*. . . seeing a crowd at a door, and enquiring the cause, (we) were told it was the theatre, and that the play was just began; in we sallied, took our places in the boxes, amidst a numerous and well-dress'd audience, and were sufficiently amused; tho it lasted too late. From a communicative neighbour, I learn'd the history of their play-house: and particularly that Mrs. Siddons made her first appearance here, in Leonora in the Padlock, with great applause. Some of the performers play'd with judgment and spirit . . . the company consist of 28 persons, including the band, and perform 3 times a week; and the gay men of the place subscribe £1.1. for a transferable ticket for 20 nights. This kept us up too late, and spoil'd our supper, for we did not get home till ½ past eleven o'clock.*

1. Inf. ex. introduction to the 1970 edition of *The Torrington Diaries*.
2. The theatre occupied the site of Nos.23 and 23a Mill Street. It opened in 1780 or earlier and closed between 1871 and 1875 though the building was not demolished until c.1890.

Next morning Byng and his friends assessed the social standing of Ludlow and visited the church and the ruined Castle:

> This is one of the best towns for a genteel family of small fortune to retire to I have ever seen; for it is cheap, well built, and clean, surrounded by a charming country; and a river; and affords a theatre, public walks, an assembly once a fortnight, and annual races.[3] The church is very large, well pew'd, and well quired . . . (the castle) exists one of the most pompous antiquities of the kingdom . . .

Later in the day Byng was entertained by Mr. P . . . l, a friend of one of his companions. This was probably Mr. John Powell (d.1799), who lived at No. 14 Corve Street from 1780, together with three daughters, a maid and a man servant.[4] He dined with Byng and his party at 3 o'clock.

> . . . this was some pleasure; but not equal to what was to follow, a grand tea-drinking at the old gentleman's house, with his daughters, and their company; I bow'd, and I bow'd, talk'd of dancing, players and puppet shews, and 'Drank my tea like a man'; when this was wearied out, a walk was proposed, tho the sun was nearly setting, and the evening so cold, that a game of cards, and a fire, had been more to my taste: now for the coquettry of the streets, and the public walks . . . Impossible to escape a return to supper, which after a long delay, and much noise of cookery, and the frying-pan, arriv'd, and then we had another course of politicks; nor could I disperse the company, till 12 o'clock at night; when we had a long crawl back to our inn.

They left Ludlow next morning, after breakfast at the *Angel* and a further social call at No. 14 Corve Street:

> At nine o'clock this morning we left Ludlow, after I had made a delicious breakfast upon buttermilk; which allways does me much good: in our way out of town we roused Mr. P . . . l (who is a civil old gentleman), and after many shakes by the hand, took our leave and the road of our departure. The castle, for some miles throws a splendour over a lovely vale . . .

*Nos. 14-15 Corve Street, built between 1771 and 1774. John Byng visited Mr. John Powell who was the tenant of No. 14 (on the left).*

3. Public walks round the Castle were laid out in 1772 (Felton, 1822, p.66). Horse races were held on two days in August from 1728; since 1739 or earlier they had been run on the Old Field at Bromfield (*V.C.H.*, 2, p.180).
4. Deduced from Easter Books, Poor Law Assessment and other Corporation papers.

John Price (1773-1801) was the author of Ludlow's first known guidebook, *The Ludlow Guide*, which he wrote at the age of about 22.[1] It was published by Henry Proctor, who had just set up as a bookseller and printer in Broad Street (see p. 83) and ran to five editions, the last published in 1808, seven years after Price's premature death.[2] Two guidebooks on Ludlow Castle also appeared about the same year and this triple event reflects a nationwide vogue for publications of this kind.[3] *The Ludlow Guide* is only a small volume (6½ in. x 4 in.) but contains 77 pages of historical and topographical information, 52 of them on Ludlow itself, the rest on 'Villages and Seats in the neighbourhood . . .'

John Price was a young man of limited means who kept his widowed mother with the fees he earned for teaching modern languages in local schools and to private pupils. He supplemented this meagre income by writing: as well as *The Ludlow Guide* he produced local guidebooks for Leominster (1795), Hereford (1796) and Worcester (1799); and there are at least two other publications to his name.[4] He is said to have opened a bookshop in Hereford but later moved to Worcester, where he died.

The memoirs of Mary Sneade (see pp.78-9) include an incidental reference to this versatile young man, who gave private tuition to her and her sister:

*They had the advantage of a French and Italian teacher who had been abroad . . . the excellent son of a poor mother. His name was Price but they called him Mons. Jean Pris. He walked across the lovely landscape every fortnight and spent 2 happy days at Bedstone. When the lesson was over . . . their father and Price discoursed on the Politics of the day and with wisdom and moderation pointed out the faults which had led to Revolution in America and France . . .[4]*

In *The Ludlow Guide* Price described the town's public buildings:

*. . . the Cross; a very handsome stone building, and very convenient for market people, being situate at the top of the Broad-street, nearly in the centre of the town. The rooms over it are appropriated to the very laudable purpose of a public school, for the instruction of 30 poor Boys and 15 poor Girls, who are clothed and have books, etc., given to them. The Boys, when at a proper age, are put out Apprentices, with a small premium, the whole supported by voluntary subscription[5] . . . The Guild-Hall is a very elegant modern building, erected at the expense of the Corporation, and situate in the Mill Street: the Hall, in which sundry meetings of the Corporation, Quarter-Sessions, etc are holden, is large and commodiously adapted to the purpose . . .[6]*

In the 1801 edition Price gave the number of houses and inhabitants in different parts of the town. He claims these figures were 'made from an exact calculation . . . purposely made for this little production', but the total number of inhabitants, 3,897, is exactly that given by the 1801 census.

|                        | Houses | Inhabs. |                                | Houses | Inhabs. |
|------------------------|--------|---------|--------------------------------|--------|---------|
| Broad Street           | 67     | 380     | High Street or the Row         | 27     | 140     |
| Lower Broad Street     | 50     | 240     | King Street, the Bull Ring, etc. | 52   | 280     |
| Brand-lane             | 14     | 57      | Corve Street and St Mary's lane | 125   | 606     |
| Bell-lane              | 15     | 60      | Upper Goalford etc.            | 61     | 262     |
| Raven-lane             | 34     | 150     | Lower Ditto                    | 77     | 376     |
| Mill-street            | 55     | 232     | Old street                     | 54     | 290     |
| Dinham etc.            | 46     | 148     | Old-Gate's Fee, etc.           | 71     | 300     |
| Castle-street          | 30     | 142     | Church-Yard, College, etc.     | 26     | 140     |

1. Vaughan, J., *The English Guidebook, c.1780-1870* (1974)
2. British Library catalogue.
3. John Thomas, *The History of Ludlow Castle* (published by himself); William Hodges, *A Historical Account of Ludlow Castle* (published by William Felton).
4. Hertfordshire County Record Office, D/EX 220 F2, p.4.
5. The Butter Cross was built 1743-6, replacing the 16th century New House. The school there was the Blue Coat Charity School, opened at the Guildhall in 1714, and re-opened over the Butter Cross in 1785.
6. A 15th century timber framed building was recased in brick in the late 1760s, to the design of Thomas F. Pritchard of Shrewsbury.

William Owen (1760-1828) was the son of Jeremiah Owen, who was a barber and hairdresser at No. 13 Broad Street.[1] William was educated at Ludlow Grammar School and in 1786 went up to London, where he later came under the patronage of Richard Payne Knight in return for 'election services' at Ludlow in 1790 by 'Old Owen and his family'.[2] He entered the Royal Academy as a student in 1791, where his earliest exhibited work was 'A View of Ludford Bridge'. His later career was primarily as a portrait painter and some of the leading men of the day were among his sitters, for example the Prime Minister William Pitt. He was elected a Royal Academician in 1806 and in 1813 became Principal Portrait Painter to the Prince Regent. Later, illness curtailed his activities, and he died tragically from accidental poisoning.

As a young man he painted this 'South West View of Ludlow Castle', which was engraved by William Bowley of Shrewsbury and used as the frontispiece to William Hodges' *An Historical Account of Ludlow Castle*, published in 1794 by William Felton (see p. 84). This publication was more successful than a rival book which came out the same year, John Thomas' *The History of Ludlow Castle*, partly because over 300 subscribers bought copies in advance, 158 of whom were resident outside Ludlow itself. As a result of this, Thomas went bankrupt and copies of his book are very scarce.[3]

Although published in 1794 the painting was made before the alterations in that year to Dinham Bridge (see pp. 80-1). It was taken from the wide path leading diagonally up Whitcliffe from the end of the bridge. There is a good view of the weir at Castle mills and of the fields in Linney, but the thickness of the vegetation on the slopes around the Castle has perhaps been exaggerated.

1. *D.N.B.*; the statement in that article that William was the son of a bookseller is incorrect.
2. Greig, J., Ed., *The Diary of Joseph Faringdon*, vol. 1 (1922), p.34.
3. Thomas Wright, *Ludlow Sketches* (1867) p.146.

Mary Sneade (1780-1858) was the second daughter of the Rev. Samuel Sneade, the Vicar of Bedstone, a rural parish 8¾ miles west of Ludlow. He and his family spent about half each year in Ludlow, then at the height of its reputation as a fashionable social centre. In 1858 Mary's daughter Ellen Olive, wife of the Rector of Ayot St Lawrence in Hertfordshire, wrote a memoir of her mother's life, using her diaries and family letters. This manuscript was used by the biographical historian, Carola Oman, as the basis for her book, *Ayot Rectory* (1965), but the quotations below are from the manuscript itself.[1] They give a delightful picture of life in Ludlow during the Napoleonic Wars as seen by the daughter of a middle class family.

The town house of the Sneades was No. 3 Brand Lane, where they were attended by a man and two maids:[2]

*'The house in Brand Lane ... had commodious offices and a good garden, extending to the ancient walls, which afforded a terraced walk with a view of the Clee Hill and Whitcliffe, whilst the sound of the river fall over Ludford and the note of the horn, as the mail coach rolled over the old bridge, charmed the ear. Delicious were the damsons*

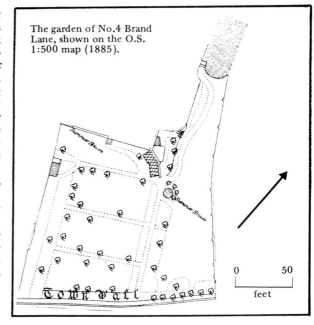

The garden of No.4 Brand Lane, shown on the O.S. 1:500 map (1885).

*and hazel nuts and nonsuch apples! Sweet the beds of thyme and chamomile! The bushes of cabbage rose & moss rose & rose de Maux'.*

Carola Oman, in her introduction, asserts that the story of Mary Sneade is often 'purest Jane Austen'; and so indeed it is![3] But Jane's heroines were less conscious of contemporary events than the Sneade sisters:

*'The horrors of the winters of 1792-93-94 in France impressed themselves strongly on mother's mind. The sound of the horn as the Mail crossed the bridge, & mounted the steep street made them tremble ... Ireland, too, was restless, and many families of position left their own land and settled in England till the storm had past. This was a source of advantage and interest to Ludlow which was a favourite resort, as well it might be ...'.[4]*

In the 18th and early 19th centuries Ludlow always had two or three academies for young ladies, one of which was that of the Misses Jordan, at No. 13 Corve Street (shown left).

*'Bessy and Mary walked every morning to a very superior school in Corve Street kept by two ladies named Jordan, who had been educated for their own gratification, but when reverses came they supported their parents by keeping a school. They were taught admirably and thoroughly by these ladies, and masters under them, to read with tone and emphasis, to write correctly, to dance & walk with grace and dignity, to work neatly, and to cultivate respectful manners to superiors in age and experience ... The Miss Jordans were religious and loved the Courts of the house of their God, and whenever an opportunity presented itself, they led their pupils to Church ...'.*

*No. 13 Corve Street, rebuilt in 1750 by Walter Griffiths, a prosperous Ludlow glover.*

1. Hertfordshire R.O., D/EX220.
2. Easter Books, 1804, etc.
3. p. 12.
4. A sidenote in the manuscript lists 'Dogan, Hills, Smith and Molyneux' as such Irish families; the last of these lived at Gravel Hill House.

*Part of a lithograph of the chancel of St Laurence's, published by Richard Jones, bookseller, in the 1850s. In spite of repairs in the 1820s, the chancel was still in a poor condition, prior to later restoration.*

Church attendance was certainly obligatory for the daughters of clergymen:

'*No gospel light shone in the noble church of St Laurence at Ludlow during this period nor for many succeeding years: the chimes of bells sounded out gloriously from the tall Tower and the Congregation assembled but without hearing the Gospel of glad tidings from the Preacher.*[5] *Pools of water filled the broken stones of the Chancel during the cold winters of that high hilly district and the careless service corresponded to the aspect of the Church . . . The daughters were regular Communicants, trembling often with cold and fearing rheumatism, for it was the custom to remain in the stalls of the desolate Chancel during the whole time of the celebration of the service. Their father directed them carefully to examine themselves, to search whether they had fallen into the great sin of Ludlow, tale bearing and scandal . . .*'.

But Ludlow in the 1790s had its gayer moments and Mary Sneade reminisced endlessly about the social delights of her youth:

'*The hours were earlier, the dress simpler, the repasts less elaborate than now a days and the enjoyment in consequence much more real. There were 2 or 3 seasons of gaiety. The summer races with a ball & public breakfast in the Castle Green, the Bailiffs' Balls in the old tumbledown Assembly Rooms, to which the neighbouring families resorted, and occasional private dances . . . At one of the Bailiffs' balls whilst going down a long country dance mother turned her foot & sprained the muscles in an agonising manner. She was borne by Herbert Oakley to a seat and then to her sedan chair . . .*'.

Mary Sneade was a popular girl and as 'the belle of Ludlow' had many local suitors, but in the end her choice was for Thomas Brown, 'an opulent East India Merchant', a business partner of Charles Rogers of Castle Square house. Their home was to be in Bath and Mary's marriage to him at St Laurence's on 24 June 1806 was, apart from precious holidays, her farewell Ludlow appearance: 'Flowers were spread beneath her feet as she walked in simple bridal costume from the Church to her carriage, and the joybells rang out merrily . . .'.

*(Right) A lithograph of Ludlow Market Hall included in Felton's* Description of the Town of Ludlow *(1822). This building was of brick and dated from 1706, when it replaced an older structure, probably timber framed. The upper storey was occupied by the 'old tumbledown Assembly Rooms' described by Mary Sneade, the largest of these being the Long Room, where the balls were held. Three chandeliers were provided in 1757 and '4 new sash windows' in 1785.*

5. There was certainly a lack of vitality at St Laurence's at this time; but it must be remembered that in its final form this assessment was made by the wife of an earnest Victorian clergyman at a period of evangelical fervour.

# DINHAM BRIDGE:
# A PICTORIAL SEQUENCE,
# 1721-1823

The frequency with which the Castle was drawn and painted has given a good pictorial record of other features in the vicinity, especially for the Castle Mills/Dinham Bridge area. The pictorial sequence below, covering the period from 1721 to 1823 and afterwards, records and explains the changes made to Dinham Bridge.

*Before 1733:* The oldest known bridge of which there is a pictorial record was built sometime in the 17th century and was called the New Bridge. It was a narrow, single-track pack bridge and could take only pedestrians and horses. Wheeled vehicles had to be drawn through the ford a few yards upstream by Castle mills. This detail from Stukeley's Prospect (see p.58) shows the bridge in 1721, with the track at the far end dropping down to the mills and then swinging back to climb up to Dinham Gate. The bridge was also shown by Dinley in 1684 and Vogelsanck and Lens in 1722. Dinham Gate, a modest castellated structure, can also be seen.

*1733-1794:* In 1733 the upper-work of the bridge was replaced in stone and brick, though still using the original piers. This engraving, published in 1813 but using a picture painted some years before, shows the humped profile of this bridge and makes it clear that the Dinham end of the bridge terminated on a narrow peninsula between the river and the mill-race. Access to the bridge, therefore, had to be up a ramp from the mill, where the leet was more easily crossed. The engraving provides interesting details of the mill buildings while the drinking cows provide a picturesque touch.

*1794-1823:* In 1794 the bridge was made usable by wheeled vehicles, following consultation with Thomas Telford, who had been appointed County Surveyor. Ten years before the narrow medieval Dinham Gate had been demolished so that larger vehicles could get down to the mills and the river, but after the loss of a waggon and a team of horses in the ford the Corporation realised that the bridge must be improved.

First, a new length of road was constructed direct from Dinham to the bridge. This was carried over the mill-race by a small arch of brick and stone which can still be seen some 8 ft. below the present road surface. William Atkins, a Corve Street builder who tendered for many Corporation contracts, estimated the cost at £48 17s. Second, the stone parapets of the bridge were levelled to the roadway and large timbers were laid across so that the road was widened by being cantilevered out over either side. A new timber parapet was then fitted to each side, so that the new structure was wide enough to take waggons and yet allow riders and pedestrians room to pass. Thomas Telford's working drawing for the arch over the mill-race shows the capped pillars still standing although the parapet has been replaced by stone; the arch supports a decorative keystone which was a quirk of the builder.

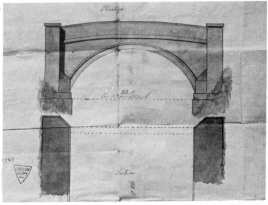

*c. 1820:* This drawing by Francis Page (see p. 85) was published as a plate in the 1852 edition of Wright's history of Ludlow but depicts the Dinham area at least 30 years before. It shows Telford's improvements of 1794, though the line of the old road can be detected from the fronts of three houses under the Castle hill. The buildings of both Castle mills can be seen and also the redundant ramp, preserved for access to the river. The toll gate across the road and the ruts made by heavy wheeled vehicles are other informative details. Further up the slope the elbow-like course of Camp Lane has been exaggerated and many of the distant buildings are very generalised; but the gable end of St Thomas's chapel has assumed its present appearance while the imposing front of Merivale House, rebuilt since Vogelsanck's panorama of 1722, can be seen on the far right.

*c.1822:* This watercolour by George Patten, A.R.A. (1801-65) is now in the Victoria and Albert Museum. Patten was later appointed portrait artist to Prince Albert. This picture shows Dinham Bridge from the south just before it was demolished and replaced by the present bridge in 1823. A carrier's waggon can be seen crossing the bridge. To the left a sinuous track climbs up Whitcliffe, though the stone slabs which caused it to be called 'the Donkey Steps' cannot be seen; donkeys allegedly used this route to take iron ore to Bringewood Forge from the Clee Hills. In the middle distance can be seen the floodable fields of Linney.

*1823 and afterwards:* The makeshift alterations of 1794 lasted for 29 years but by 1823 the whole structure was considered 'insufficient, inconvenient and dangerous' and the Shrewsbury architect, John Straphen, the designer of Lord Hill's monument, was asked to submit a design for the shapely three-arched bridge which still stands today. It is, however, on a different alignment; the footings of the old bridge can still be seen in summer in the riverbed downstream, obliquely to the line of the present structure.

William Mavor (1758-1837) was one of many travellers who visited 'picturesque' Wales in the early 19th century and later published accounts of their journeys. Several such travellers included Ludlow in their itineraries but most of the descriptions are repetitive and rely heavily on earlier publications. In contrast, Mavor's account of 'A Tour through Wales in the summer of 1805' is based entirely on first hand observation. It was published privately in 1806 but found a wider circulation in 1809 when it was incorporated in the third edition of *The British Tourist's or Traveller's Pocket Companion*, which was edited by Mavor himself.

William Fordyce Mavor was a Scotsman who became a schoolmaster in Woodstock, first as private tutor to the children of the 3rd Duke of Marlborough, later as Headmaster of Woodstock Grammar School. He was Mayor of Woodstock 10 times and also its Rector from 1810 until his death. He wrote 37 books, including *New Description of Blenheim* (1793), one of the first guide books to a 'stately home', and the very successful *The English Spelling Book* (1801).[1]

He and his companions approached from the north and spent the afternoon and evening 'viewing the beauties of the place'. They stayed at an unnamed inn and left for Worcester early the next morning.

*The town of Ludlow stands on an eminence . . . It is washed on two sides by the Teme, over which a handsome wooden bridge on brick arches is thrown.[2] The situation is universally and deservedly admired . . . the inhabitants amount to little less than 4,000 persons. Indeed many respectable families reside here . . . For Centuries it has been a place of some consequence . . .*

*The castle, still an object of great interest, was long the residence of the Lords President of Wales. The Mask of Comus was composed by Milton . . . and acted here about the year 1634 . . . The ruins of this magnificent pile cannot be contemplated even at this period without admiration; and I was happy to find that Lord Powis, the lessee of the Prince of Wales, entertains a due sense of the value of his possessions, by saving it from wanton dilapidation. Round the castle the most charming walks are conducted on terraces, one above another!*

*Ludlow contains four principal streets . . . The houses are generally built of brick and tiled and the streets are clean and well paved. The want of slating, however, is a considerable drawback on the beauty of the place. Some of the old houses are of frame-work, painted black, with the interstices white, a stile of building still to be seen in many other places, but rapidly disappearing, as repairs and improvements become necessary. The shops make a handsome appearance; and the inns possess superior accommodation. The manufacture of gloves employs many hands; and much business is done in paper-making and tanning.[3] It is not, however, a commercial town, as many of the inhabitants live on their fortunes . . .*

*. . . we sat down to dinner at seven o'clock, and afterwards took a perambulation of a part of the town we had not previously visited. Here we saw two lofty May-poles, hung from within two feet of the ground to the top, with garlands of various coloured paper, very tastefully disposed; and on entering we learnt that Whitsun sports are usually celebrated with much glee by the young people of both sexes. Whitsun ales are not unusual in some parts of the kingdom; but I have never before observed such gay poles, which must have required abundant labour and ingenuity to execute and adorn.[4]*

A view down Old Street towards Holdgate Fee, shown on a Valentine's postcard c.1910. This was one of the parts of the town where Maypole dancing occurred and may have been the area visited by Mavor and his companion. In the Middle Ages this and other parts of Ludlow owed allegiance to the Lord of Holdgate, a manor in Corvedale.

1. *D.N.B.*; Vaughan (1974), pp.52,55.
2. This was Dinham bridge, where a wooden superstructure had been added to earlier foundations in 1794. See p.80.
3. See p.84 for Ludlow's glove making industry. Woodstock, Mavor's home town, was also an important glove making centre, e.g. Knight's *Cyclopedia of the Industry of all Nations* (1851) names Worcester, Woodstock, Yeovil, Leominster, Ludlow and London as 'the great seats of the leather glove manufacture in England'.
4. Burne, p.360, confirms the importance of Maypoles at Ludlow: *Up to 1840 a Maypole was reared regularly by the New Bridge at the foot of Whitcliffe, and twenty years later one was annually set up on a particular spot in the Holdgate Fee—a wide open street outside the old walls of the town. The last one was reared there in 1864 and remained until it decayed away in 1876 . . . the old open-air dances were still carried on till the year 1860 or thereabouts, in Holdgate Fee and Upper and Lower Gaolford. 'I have seen', says the gentleman who is my informant, 'as many as twenty fiddlers, and the dancing couples reaching the whole length of the street.'*

*In Ludlow, as might reasonably be expected, there are a reading society, a coffee-room and a respectable bookseller's shop and printing office, conducted by Mr. Proctor, who appears to be a man of taste and information.*[5]

Mavor goes on to describe 'various seats' in the locality and concludes with his attendance at morning prayers at St Laurence's Parish Church, just before leaving for Tenbury, where he and his friends had breakfast:

*Being ready before my friends and hearing the bells ringing for prayers at six o'clock I went into the church and inspected its contents. The painted glass is in the best stile of colouring but the designs, which never could have possessed much merit, are further deteriorated by broken panes, whose loss has been supplied by common glass. The interior of the church is handsomely fitted up and is extremely capacious. An elegant organ is erected over the entrance into the chancel . . . A few old men and women, perhaps not exceeding twelve in all, composed the congregation. I fear that too frequent service in the church tends to lessen the veneration of the people for this sacred duty. Where prayers are read thrice a day, it is too frequently considered a routine business, both by the minister and his flock.*

*Henry Proctor's pleasing trade card was used as a frontispiece to the second edition of* The Ludlow Guide, *published in 1797 (see p. 76).*

5. Henry Proctor, son of the Vicar of Orleton, set up his business at what is now No. 13 Broad Street in 1794 but in 1803 moved to what is now No. 10 Broad Street. Wright (1867, p. 147) describes him as *the head bookseller of the town . . . the bookseller and printer of the aristocracy of Ludlow and its neighbourhood.*

William Felton (1769-1852) was a native of Ludlow who operated a printing and bookselling business on the site of what is now No. 18 King Street. This opened in 1794 and continued until his death.[1] During the years preceeding the Reform Act of 1832 he was the town's leading radical and many of his publications were political. A memorial in the north transept of the Parish Church eulogises him as 'a strenuous supporter of Civil and Religious Liberty'.

In 1811 he published *A Description of the Town of Ludlow with a Historical Account of the Castle*, which ran to several editions. The first edition had 144 pages but by 1822 these had increased to 208. In 1811 he gave 15 pages to the church, 42 to the Castle, 50 to the rest of the town and 37 to 'the environs', mainly to 'the seats' of gentlemen. The section on the town includes a short account of 'Trade and Manufactures', especially glove making:

*. . . the glove line has been brought of late years into great repute and perfection and the number of men, women and children employed in it amounts to several hundreds. This manufactory is, undoubtedly, beneficial to the town at large, because a great number of the persons employed in sewing gloves might otherwise probably be under the necessity of requiring parochial assistance . . .*[2]

In each edition Felton published up-to-date details of 'Posts, Mail and Stage Coaches'. In 1822 there were 27 coaches out of Ludlow each week during the summer.[3] Shortened timetables of two of these are given below:

| The Aurora from the Angel Inn every day at 3 o'clock in the afternoon to: | |
|---|---|
| Tenbury | 9 miles |
| Worcester by 7 o'clock and start at 5 o'clock the following morning | 25 miles |
| Oxford by half-past eleven | 55 miles |
| London at six the same evening | 54 miles |
| Total | 143 miles |

| The Leek Post Coach goes (in the summer months) from the Crown Hotel at 4 o'clock every Wednesday morning through: | |
|---|---|
| Bishop's Castle | 17 miles |
| Newtown | 18 miles |
| Machynlleth | 30 miles |
| Aberystwith the same evening | 26 miles |
| Total | 91 miles |

Transport for goods and for poorer passengers was by waggon,[4] e.g.

**Robert's London Waggon,** *starts from his warehouse Corve Street, Ludlow, every Monday night, and arrives at the George Inn, Smithfield, London, on Saturday, about 1 o'clock: sets out from thence every Sunday morning, and arrives in Ludlow the Friday evening following.*

**Weaver and Hughes's Waggons to and from Bewdley,** *several times in the week each, convey parcels which come by water to Birmingham, Stourport, and Bewdley, from London, Bristol and other parts of England.*

Felton included a number of illustrations in each edition. These were lithographs made from drawings by local artists. The 1822 edition contains a series by Francis Page, a professional drawing master who lived in Mill Street.

1. Wright, 1867, p.147.
2. p.40. Documents confirm that at this time Ludlow had 12 master glovers, who employed men to cut the leather and women and children to stitch the gloves, the latter usually working in their own homes. In 1813 720 people were employed and some 660,000 gloves were produced. The industry declined sharply after 1815, due to competition from cheaper products mad abroad and in the East Midlands.
3. pp.75-6.
4. p. 77. Robert's warehouse was at Nos. 140 and 141 Corve Street, the premises later occupied by the Ludlow Water Company.

This shows that the ground floor arches of the Butter Cross were still open and that the timber-framed buildings at the top of Broad Street were masked by plaster. Most of the double-jettied building on the corner (now No. 20 King Street/No. 1 Broad Street) was occupied by Mrs. Hughes, the widow of a master glover; but the small shop on the corner was one of a row of King Street premises leased by William Felton himself. No.2 Broad Street, with the twin gables facing the artist, was occupied by James Noakes, grocer. The picture also gives a unique glimpse of shops on the north side of King Street prior to 19th century rebuilding. There is a clear view of the three-bay building (now the site of Barclays Bank) which was owned and occupied by John Smith, a leading ironmonger who later became Mayor; while to the left is one bay of the property of Thomas Hotchkiss, saddler, which was refronted and raised in 1829.

This is the earliest known view looking down Broad Street from above the Broad Gate. It shows the street dropping steeply through the gateway, prior to alterations made on the advice of Thomas Telford in 1829. The two trees are an important part of the townscape but the one on the left, a massive horse chestnut, was to achieve much greater height before it was cut down in 1922. The house fronts are little different from those of today, though alterations had occurred on some of them since Samuel Scott made his painting in 1766. The terraced walk in front of Nos.35 and 36, raised by Thomas Dunne of Gatley Park in 1757, is still open at the far end and steps probably led down to street level, as shown on a picture taken from the Broad Gate c.1810. Annuitants and professional families occupied most of these large houses, e.g. Henry Lloyd, a lawyer, had moved into Broad Gate in 1814, while No.31, the five-bay house on the left, was the home of John Hutchins, a gentleman of means from Somerset (see p.99).

Joseph Bullock was a weaver who lived in Bell Lane, though he was born in Leominster. In 1818 he wrote a poem, *The Beauties of Ludlow*, which was printed by William Felton and sold for one shilling.[1] The poem is 250 lines long and is a topographical description of Ludlow, with occasional diversions. It is badly written and mostly doggerel but is not without historical interest, especially the last 50 lines which describe the ceremony of Bailiffs' Change. The High Bailiff, one of the 12 aldermen, and the Low Bailiff, one of the 25 councillors, were elected for a year of office.[2] The change took place on 28 October, the festival of St Simon and St Jude, and was the major social event of the year. Bullock says that he has attended for 42 years but his social position makes it unlikely that he was a guest. His interest in the dancing suggests that he was a member of the band.

> *The Corporation both wealthy and great Invite all their friends to their annual treat,*
> *A sumptious dinner, drest in the first stile, The company all, in general smile,*
> *At seeing the tables so very well stor'd With all the good things the season affords,*
> *Fish, fowl, and flesh, on the table are plac'd, And all the first dishes with ornaments grac'd,*
> *Nice jellies are put upon each glass stand, With puddings and pies on every hand,*
> *Numberless bottles of good wine are there, A sumptious and delicious fare,*
> *An agreeable desert next comes in, Dinner being over the toasts begin,*
> *Mirth and good humour we constantly see, 'Till the change takes place and they go to tea,*
> *By and by, they return, the evening to spend, Where of drinking and toasting there is no end,*
> *But after a time you enjoy a good song, And some of them stay I can't tell how long,*
> *Others go home to prepare for the ball, Where the respectable families all,*
> *With Lords and Ladies far and near, Honour the Bailiffs in every year.*
> *The Ladies and Gentlemen at the ball meet Their Worships and Ladies to congratulate.*
> *'Tis forty-two years I have attended The ball-room of Ludlow, which is as splendid*
> *As ever it was in any past years, With full as much beauty and grace it appears,*
> *Richly attir'd in the fashion of the day, The music attending the dances to play,*
> *Which are danc'd much better than in former days, The improvements in dancing merit great praise*
> *The steps are all done both graceful and neat, The figures also which make it complete.*
> *The whole with great taste, elegance and ease, The band all the time endeavouring to please.*
> *The dancing continues until about two, When the ladies withdraw and a scene quite new,*
> *Immediately follows: for in walks Jerry,[3] Who never has fail'd to make them all merry;*
> *He makes them to sing and pass a good joke And sometimes to take to their pipes and smoke;*
> *Toasting and singing still keeps them alive 'Till the chimes go four, or the clock strikes five,*
> *And some of them later, almost 'till seven, May we giddy mortals be all forgiven.*

*A view westwards along Bell Lane, looking towards Mill Street. This was one of the cross lanes of the 12th century planned town. The three-storey houses on the right, built in the 1830s, are known locally as 'Bribery Row'. This dates from the fiercely contested elections after 1832 when they were leased to tenants on condition that they voted Whig.*

1. *Herefordshire Tracts*, Vol.15 (1818).
2. In 1818 21 members of the Corporation lived outside Ludlow, including eight members of the Clive family. The rest were local professional men and a handful of the richer tradesmen.
3. A silver gallon tankard belonging to the Corporation.

*The Free Grammar School Ludlow.*

This engraving, by Thomas Saunders of Shrewsbury, comes from a small textbook, *Latin Prosody*, written in 1800 by Jean Doudouit, a French emigré priest who taught French and Latin at Ludlow Grammar School. The school at that time was in 'a very flourishing condition', for as well as teaching the Ludlow boys as foundationers the masters took paying boarders, some of them the sons of county gentry in the Ludlow area but others from as far away as North Wales and Gloucestershire.[1]

The picture shows a medieval stone range parallel to the street. In the Middle Ages this was the town house of the Cheneys of Cheney Longville (eight miles north west of Ludlow), an influential local family closely associated with the Castle. The arched doorway to the screens passage can be seen with the hall above lit by two pairs of lancet windows while the service end was below. The Grammar School moved here from a building near the Church in 1527. The Head or 'Chiefe Maister' taught the older boys in the former hall and the Usher took the younger boys in the service wing. Later in the century the parlour at the top end of the hall was rebuilt as the Headmaster's house, the gable end of which can be seen on the picture. The roof was raised in 1685 and the dormer windows were inserted to light the dormitories, where up to 50 boys were at times accommodated.

A view looking south from Castle Square, sometime before 1840.[2] Mill Street, one of the main residential streets of the town, was curiously neglected by artists and photographers but this picture shows that the upper western side was already much as it is today. At the top is Castle Lodge, the home of Dr. Babington in the early 19th century. Below, the three Georgian houses erected in 1740 by Henry Karver, an attorney, can be seen while beyond is the timber-framed *Hop Pole Inn*, with its jetty and twin dormers. After that the modern sequence of properties can be seen as far as and beyond the Guildhall.

On the left is the pleasing facade of the *White Horse Inn*, demolished in 1840 to make way for the new Assembly Rooms. The building became an inn about 1730. Before that it was occupied by a series of important tradesmen, e.g. Mr. John Reynolds, mercer (d.1676), who was twice Bailiff. The picture suggests that the timber framed structure once had a jetty which had been under-pinned with brick or stone walls. The large number of chimney stacks is a feature of the building and reaffirms the documentary record of 11 hearths in 1663.

The end of the old Market Hall can just be seen on the far left of the picture (see p. 79).

1. Lloyd (1977), pp.70, 92, 107.
2. Jones, E., *Pen Sketches of Old Ludlow* (1912-3).

An anonymous article entitled 'Reminiscences of an Old Inhabitant', published in *The Ludlow Advertiser* in January 1903, gives delightful anecdotes of life in Ludlow, many of them childhood memories from the second and third decades of the 19th century.

The author was almost certainly Mary Jones (1809-1906), who was aged 93 when the articles were written and the town's oldest resident. She was born in September 1809, the youngest of 11 children of Edward and Anne Collier, three of whom died as infants. Edward Collier was a gardener and also licensee of the *King's Arms* where the family lived, in what is now No. 41 Bull Ring.[1] In later life she married John Jones, a local farmer, and after his death was matron of Lane's Asylum in Old Street, then used as an almshouse.[2] She ended her days in comparative luxury, living at 'Bringewood' in Gravel Hill, Ludlow's most elegant Victorian suburb.[3] This was the home of her son, Edmund Jones (1848-1914), who was a grocer at No. 15 High Street from *c.*1878.[4] Edmund Jones was a thoughtful and prolific writer of newspaper articles on local history, which were reprinted as a series of booklets shortly before his death.[5] It is almost certain that he helped his nonagenarian mother to write her article.

'I was born in the first decade of the last century, and have lived in Ludlow all my life. My earliest recollections carry me back to the time when conversation was frequent among my elders about the doings at Dinham House during the period (1810-1811) that Lucien Bonaparte and his family were imprisoned there. Their habits and social customs, and the hurried manner of their conveyance through the country to Ludlow, found employment for the tongues of grown-up people for a long time. A few years later, Ludlow was beside itself with joy over the victory at Waterloo, and I can still see in mind's eye the bonfires burning at the Market Hall, the Cross, the Bull Ring and the Linney turn in Corve Street, where an effigy of the great Napoleon was finally burned after being ignominiously drawn through the principal streets on a cart. Dinham House was then an occasional residence of Lord Clive, and the arrival of the family was always celebrated by a peal of church bells. The main streets of the town were very lively with wheel traffic, the coming and going of light and heavy coaches being a matter of daily occurrence. Oysters and other fish were brought to the town from the Welsh coast on horseback, and their sale at the Fish Bench which stood at the back of the old Market Hall, would be proclaimed by the Town Crier. Newspapers were brought in in the same manner. The *Crown*, now a chemist's shop in Broad Street, and the *Angel*, were the chief points of arrival and departure of the daily coaches, and in the summer months seaside requirements were met by a bi-weekly coach starting from the *Crown* at 4 o'clock in the morning.[6] Robert's London waggons would start from the warehouse in Corve-street (now Bluck's ironmongery stores) on Monday mornings carrying goods and passengers, and reaching London the following Saturday.[7] Mail coaches covered the distance in two days and I remember travelling about eighty years ago by the *Aurora*, leaving the *Angel* one Saturday afternoon, staying the night in Worcester, starting from thence at 5 o'clock Sunday morning, through Oxford at midday when the collegians were coming out of church and passing Tyburn turnpike when the London bells were chiming for evening service.

'I have a vivid recollection of being taken to the Parish Church one Sunday when very little, to see a man doing penance for some offence; he walked up and down the middle

*Lucien Bonaparte, a younger brother of Napoleon, was held on parole at Dinham House from late in 1810 until 1 July 1811, following capture at sea whilst seeking refuge in the United States. He was accompanied by his wife, their seven children and 23 servants and attendants.*

1. Inferred from Easter rate books, poor law assessments and other documents.
2. Birth certificate of Edmund Jones, 6 December 1848; 1881 census returns.
3. Kelly's *Directory of Shropshire*, 1900, p. 129.
4. Various trade directories.
5. Edmund Jones, *Pen Sketches of Ludlow*, 1912; second series, 1913.
6. The *Crown* occupied what are now Nos. 56 and 58 Broad Street.
7. Nos. 140 and 141 Corve Street, later the premises of the Ludlow Motor Company.

*Dinham House, which was built c.1716 and extended in 1748. It was used as a town house by some of the leading families in the district, including the Knights of Downton (originally ironmasters), the Johnes of Croft Castle and the Earl of Powis, who rented it to Lucien Bonaparte.*

aisle with a white covering, repeating certain words. I frequently saw burials within the walls of the sacred edifice, one in particular I remember in 1821, in St John's Chapel.[8] I have also seen interments in the porch. There was no service at night on Sundays, and in the afternoons during the winter light was supplied from chandeliers hung at various points. The streets of the town had oil lamps, and I can still call to mind the hourly cry of the night-watchman, 'past 2 o'clock and a starlight morning'; when the nights were dark they would be described as cloudy. I have known wheat at 30s per bushel and the quality of bread so bad that a slice from a loaf would adhere to the wall if thrown at it. Salt was 4½d per lb., tea 8s to 10s per lb., loaf sugar 1s, brown sugar 8d. Middle-class children were not allowed tea more than once a day; breakfast consisted of oatmeal and milk served up in the same apartment, but not at the same table as their parents. In the spring and summer months eggs could be purchased at 30 for a shilling, fresh butter 8d per lb. At the Winter Fair large quantities of Welsh butter and cheese would be exposed for sale in Castle-Street. There was also a large Hop Fair in September

*Linney Turn, where Napoleon's effigy was burnt in 1815. This was an ancient meeting place and the site of a small suburban market. The buildings on the left, now Nos. 38/39 Corve Street, were once glovers' cottages, with a through workshop above. They were built in the early 19th century on the site of the medieval chapel of St Leonard. The building on the far right is all that remains of premises occupied by builders throughout the 19th century; most of these were removed when Coronation Avenue was constructed in 1937.*

8. Probably the burial of Elizabeth Dyke in 1821, when a white stone was inserted in an older memorial slab. Anne Dyke was a witness to the wedding of Mary Jones's parents in 1779.

held in Mill-street. On fair days the Town Crier would make a proclaimation warning the inhabitants to guard their property from thieves, and at 7 o'clock in the evening the great bell in the church would be rung. Glove-making was a very extensive industry in Ludlow, until ruined by the introduction of foreign goods.

'I remember the building of New Bridge and saw the first stone being laid by the Hon. R. Clive in 1823. The old bridge was a wooden one on stone piers. It was not strong enough to carry heavy waggons. The river was fordable at the Castle Mill and the common was open to the water's edge. I remember on the site of Friar's Terrace, in Old-street, an old round tower, the remains of the Old Gate. It formed part of an inn known as the *Mug House*, afterwards the *Dog*, at the back of the premises being a cock pit. I have many times from an upper window looked down on to this pit to see battles fought. Thirteen of these battles were called a 'main'. Opposite this tower, and adjoining the Workhouse entrance, were the parish stocks, often occupied by drunkards. These stocks were afterwards removed to the Market Hall. At the back of the Workhouse was the House of Correction, with a very formidable door, guarded by

(*Above*) This drawing, placed in a scrap album in 1867, shows the two buildings which were used as the Workhouse.[9] The left hand house is a 15th or early 16th century structure astride the town wall; it once extended further into the street. The right hand house was built in the 16th century but was refronted in 1621. In the late 17th century both properties were acquired by the trustees of Thomas Lane (d. 1676) and were used as a Workhouse and House of Correction until 1837. After 1837 they were known as Lane's Asylum and were used as an almshouse.

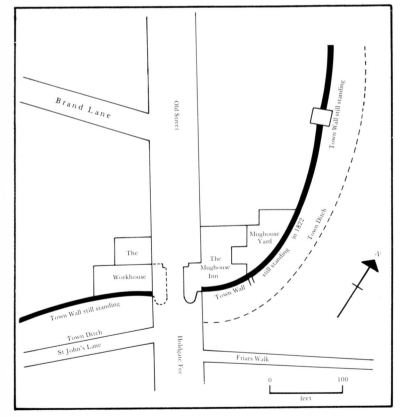

(*Left*) A map to show the vicinity of Old Gate in 1822, before the present Friars' Terrace and adjoining premises were built.[10] The eastern drum tower of Old Gate was still standing and formed part of the Mughouse Inn, as described by Mary Jones. The western drum tower had been demolished by 1780 but its supposed outline is shown by a broken line. Corporation leases make it clear that there were once rooms over the gateway, as in the other major gates of the town. The two properties constituting the Workhouse are also shown.

9. *Some Account of the Visit of the British Archaeological Association held in Ludlow in the County of Salop, 29 July, 1867* (1867), facing p. 1. Local Studies Library, Shrewsbury.
10. Based on a Ludlow Corporation lease, 28 October, 1822 to William Davenport, yeoman (SRO 356, box 356).

*The* Feathers *in 1822, drawn by John Buckler (1779-1851), an architectural artist with a high reputation for accuracy.* [11] *The doorway is under the protruding entrance bay, in the position described by Mary Jones; while the 'shoeing smithy' occupied the former premises of the Griffin, a late medieval inn which was rebuilt in the 1670s.*

*The* Feathers *some years later, as shown on a lithograph by John Clayton (d. 1864), a Hereford architect.* [12] *The doorway has been moved to a central position and the smithy has been rebuilt as part of a stuccoed three storey block; but the 'electioneering balcony' has not yet been erected. The lithograph was published in 1846 but may have been drawn some years before.*

numerous bolts and bars. In the centre was a small iron grating—an opening for the purpose of giving food to the prisoners. I have often seen men and women lodged in this dark cell. It had no window. At this time the front of the *Feathers* differed from its present appearance. The entrance was a little lower down, and adjoining the end of the house was a shoeing smithy open to the street. There was no balcony over the front door; it was afterwards constructed to meet electioneering requirements. As time rolled on the old coaching days disappeared, the iron horse came upon the scene, bringing in its train new men and new manners, but to one who has lived through all these changes there is still much pleasure in looking back upon the good old times.

*This is the earliest known picture of the railway, which was opened between Shrewsbury and Ludlow in 1851 and was extended to Hereford in 1852. It was probably painted by William Gwynn, but lacks the quality of his early work (see pp. 92-3). The railway line can be seen on an embankment towards the back of the picture. The* Queen's Arms, *opened in 1850, occupies an island site in the middle distance. The landlord, Richard Bird, operated a haulage business and one of his waggons is in front of the inn. Before the railway was built the New Road turnpike up Gravel Hill passed to the right of the inn and the road to Fishmoor went to the left; but to save expense, only the latter was bridged and a detour had to be made to reach New Road. The* Mitre Inn, *which was in Stanton Lacy parish, can be seen on the left, together with its complex of outbuildings.*

11.   BL, Add. Mss 36437, fo. 185.
12    Clayton (1846), plate 12.

William Gwynn (1782-c.1860) was a Ludlow-born artist of considerable talent. He was one of the twin sons of John and Anne Gwynn, whose circumstances were modest but not poor. Though John Gwynn is described as a labourer, he was able to live as a tenant at No.103-4 Corve Street, the spacious timber framed building later known as Tudor Guest House.[1] As a young man William Gwynn spent time in London, where his eldest son was born in 1812. It is possible, therefore, that he can be identified with the William Gwynn of London who exhibited portraits at the Royal Academy between 1807 and 1817.[2] He maintained his contact with Ludlow, where his parents lived until 1820, and was responsible for illustrations of the town published in 1807, 1811 and 1812; and a beautiful watercolour of the Vogelsanck panorama (see pp. 62-3) prepared before 1827. His 'North east view of Ludlow', published in 1811, is the Frontispiece, while his superb print of Corve Street, published in 1812, is reproduced below. Then, as now, the scene was dominated by the imposing profile of the Parish Church but the human figures add interest and catch the serene mood of a summer evening while the architectural details are historically very informative.

On the left are Nos.111 and 112, which together had constituted a property known as 'the Great House', associated with prosperous cloth manufacturers in the 15th and 16th centuries and then with the Powises, an important family of tanners. By 1812 the northern part had been completely rebuilt, while a joiner, George Bowen, occupied the older, timber framed portion; most of the facade had been rendered with stucco, though the joists of the late medieval jetty were still visible. Beyond is the modest frontage of what is now the grandiose Stone House (No.113), which was rebuilt in opulent style in the mid-19th century. Until his death in 1805 this was the house of Samuel Monger, a master glover. The larger house further up the road is the present No. 114.

On the right we catch a glimpse of the chimney to No.33 and a gate which looks very much like that to the present stone mason's yard. The wall beyond, with a sharp kink in the alignment which has since been straightened out, is that of the Friars, which was at this time pasture and orchard but was formerly the site of the Carmelite Friary. The entrance was through a little gateway hidden by the kink which was later moved to Linney; for the present archway into what became St Leonard's churchyard was not built until 1824. Beyond, somewhat foreshortened, are Nos. 14-32 Corve Street, many of which are still as depicted. The further of the two timber framed houses is the *Eagle and Child* tavern, an inn since the late 17th century, which was subsequently refaced in brick.

1. Easter Books and poor rate assessments.
2. Foster, J.J., *A Dictionary of Painters and Miniaturists* (1926), p. 134.

Gwynn moved back to Ludlow in the 1830s and lived in Corve Street for the rest of his life, first at No.100, two doors below his childhood home. He advertised himself as an artist but it is probable that his services were mostly employed for portraiture and a number of cameo miniatures and small equestrian watercolours of good quality survive in the Ludlow area. The only known topographical work of this period, 'View of the Inner Court of Ludlow Castle', is reproduced above. This was clearly a private venture for it is inscribed 'Drawn and Published by Wm. Gwynn, Corve Street, Ludlow, Salop May 6th. 1838'. While his style seems to have become a little quaint and stereotyped his flair for the unusual and exciting in views is still apparent and the print must have caused some admiration when it first appeared.

The print shows the buildings of the inner bailey but adds little to what can be learnt from earlier and more detailed pictures. Of much greater interest is the landscape in the middle distance, sweeping round from Whitcliffe and Bringewood Chase on the left to Whitbatch and Gravel Hill on the right. In the distance can be seen the outlines of the Long Mynd, the indented View Edge and the twin summits of the Brown Clee. On the left in the middle distance are the woods at the northern end of Whitcliffe, with fir trees above the sheer quarry face, just as they are today. The road sweeps round the bottom of the hill while Halton Lane rises at an angle across the landscape towards Oakly Park, the residence of Lord Clive. In the centre the River Teme and Linney fields are hidden by the Castle towers but to the right there is a clear view of Gravel Hill, which seems to climb up steeply from above the roofs of Corve Street.

The long building at the top must be the Ludlow Union Workhouse, which was not completed until 1839, while to the right can be seen Gravel Hill House, built in the 18th century.

After 1850 the advent of cheaper photography took much of Gwynn's trade and he worked principally as a sign-painter while his son, who lived in Old Street, was a painter and gilder. In 1860 however, aged 78, he published a west view of St Laurence's to commemorate the restoration of the west windows and the porch, and its inscription can be his swan song:

*To The Subscribers to the Restoration Fund this Print is dedicated by their very respectful Servant Willm. Gwynn Senr. Ludlow, Published July 20th. 1860.*

Thomas Griffiths (1764-1852) was in business in Ludlow as an auctioneer and printer from 1794 until c.1860, though in later years much of the work was undertaken by his son.[1] His first premises were at a property later called 10 Broad Street but he soon vacated these to Henry Proctor and moved to the Bull Ring, first to No.3, later to Nos.41-2, part of the building known as Imperial Chambers. He printed a wide range of booklets and papers, much of it ephemeral such as play-bills, advertisements and invitations, but of great interest to historians; and he fortunately placed a copy of each in large scrapbooks, of which two have survived, covering the periods 1816-26 and 1839-44.[2]

One of these documents was a list of *Names of the Persons relieved as Paupers* by the parish of St Laurence's, Ludlow, up to 24 October 1817. There are 238 names on the list but many of these had large families, so that altogether about 450 persons are represented, about 10% of the town's population, which was 4,150 in 1811 but climbed to 4,820 by 1821.[3] The figures are a salutory correction to the memoirs of Mary Sneade and her kind (see pp.78-9).

1817 was a particularly bad year for Ludlow for the post-war economic depression felt by the whole country was accentuated locally by the slump in the glove trade, partly due to competition in foreign markets by French exports. Only 67 occupations are listed but it is no coincidence that 26 of these were glovecutters or gloveresses and a further 9 were leatherparers.

| Name and Age | | Trade and No. in Family | | Residence | per week | Observations |
|---|---|---|---|---|---|---|
| John Davies | 78 | Shoemaker | 2 | Gaolford | 3s. 0d. | |
| Thomas Hayes | 70 | Labourer | 2 | Noakes's Yard | 5s. 0d. | Wife confi'd to bed |
| Richard Thomas | 60 | Leatherparer | 5 | Dinham | 5s. 0d. | Wife blind |
| Mary Smith, widow | 27 | Gloveress | 4 | Gaolford | 6s. 0d. | |
| William Matthews | 56 | Plaisterer | 7 | New Bridge | 2s. 0d. | |
| Elizabeth Butcher | 40 | Gloveress | 5 | Dean's Yard | 3s. 0d. | Husband transported |
| Elizabeth Williams, widow | 78 | | | Almshouse | 1s. 0d. | |
| John Probert | 62 | Glovecutter | 4 | Gaolford | 2s. 0d. | |
| Ursula Holt's child | 5 | | | Tower Street | 2s. 0d. | At Thomas Griffiths's |
| John Whitehouse | 40 | Sweep | 4 | Frog Lane | 2s. 0d. | |
| Margaret Tongue | 21 | Gloveress | | Gaolford | 2s. 0d. | Pregnant |
| Catherine Williams | 29 | Gloveress | | Worcester | 1s. 0d. | Husband left |
| William Tongue's child | 6 | | | Bull Ring | 1s. 6d. | Father transported |

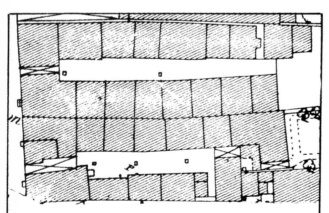

*Back building on the east side of Old Street, shown on the 1:500 O.S. map of 1885. The upper yard was Noakes's Yard and the lower Dean's Yard, after early 19th century owners.*

Not all the households are located and about 50 are extra-parochial but the remaining 144 are heavily concentrated in certain parts of the town. There was gross over-crowding in the courts and alleys which resulted from back-building on the long burgage plots of the original town plan. Forty five of the relieved persons were in Galdeford and its yards, 19 in Old Street, 15 in Lower Broad Street, 14 in Corve Street and 11 in Holgate Fee, while eight were in the Almshouses and 38 in the Workhouse. On the other hand there were only four in Dinham, three in Broad Street, one in Linney and none at all in Mill Street or Castle Street.

1.  Wright (1867), p.147.
2.  Now in Ludlow Museum.
3.  *V.C.H.* 2, p.224.

John Wood (c.1780-1847) was a land surveyor from Edinburgh, who made a large number of plans of Scottish and English towns.[1] Ludlow was surveyed in 1835, the same year as Bridgnorth, Cirencester, Ellesmere, Monmouth and Stroud. Although some details are inaccurate, e.g. the property boundaries between Corve Street and Linney, this is the earliest-known large scale map of Ludlow and gives valuable information about the extent of the built up area and about land ownership.

The map is tinted and shows the four historic wards of the town: Castle ward, Broad Street ward, Old Street and Galdeford ward and Corve Street ward. Only Corve Street ward, shaded brown, shows up clearly on the black and white reproduction below but the boundaries between the other wards can be discerned. The parish boundary can be traced, except in the south east, where it followed Weeping Cross Lane which is just off the map. An outlier of Stanton Lacy is visible in the north west, strengthening the evidence that the new town of Ludlow was created out of that parish.

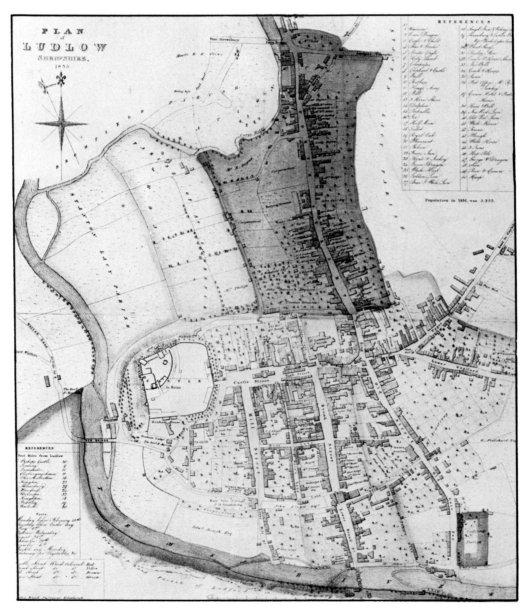

1. Mair,D.G., *The Early Maps of Scotland* (1983), pp.282-3.

Henry Bryan Ziegler (1798-1874) belonged to a well known family of European painters, but he himself was probably born in England. He had a successful career as a landscape painter, including a period of patronage by Queen Adelaide and other members of the royal family; but in later years he felt that 'his occupation had gone' because of the development of photography and he became a recluse.[1]

He painted in many parts of Great Britain and Europe but had a particular fondness for the Welsh border. He first came to the area when Thomas Knight employed him to sketch the scenery round Downton Castle and at this time he met his future wife who came from Leintwardine. He never lived permanently in Ludlow but he died in the town whilst visiting relatives in 1874 and is buried in St Leonard's churchyard.

*This picture of* Lower Broad Street *was painted in 1826, a few years after the Regency extension had been built in front of the western drum tower of the Broad Gate. The portrayal of the coach and horses, with the postboy and his horn, is one of the best pictures we have of Ludlow's 'coaching days', though it is unlikely that the little group of bystanders would have been so disinterested when the coach had just passed them. Though there are some large Georgian houses this was one of the poorer parts of the town in the early 19th century and overcrowding and poor sanitation were to be found in the courts and alleys leading off the main street. The range over the Broad Gate, the large chestnut tree (see p. 85) and the roofline of Brand House make an effective background to the central part of the picture.*

*This detail from* A South East View of Ludlow, *published in 1826, shows some of the properties on the west side of Lower Broad Street, including the huddle of buildings round the mill on the far right, one of a series of mills on this site going back to the 13th century. To the left are long cloths, fastened to racks by teynter hooks, which are being dried after fulling. Until its abrupt decline after 1600 cloth manufacture had been the basis of Ludlow's economy but in 1826 the only producer was William Evans who occupied the large premises behind the mill.*

# JOHN BUCKLER (1822)
# AND JOHN CLAYTON, c.1840

John Buckler (1770-1851) and John Clayton (d.1861) were practising architects who also became architectural artists.[1] John Buckler has a high reputation for accuracy and the vast collection of his drawings in the British Library is an important source for the study of English buildings. The Ludlow drawings suggest the use of a camera obscura. Clayton, who first practised at Hereford but later moved to London, is less well known, though his detailed drawings of Wren's churches won him the premium of the Royal Academy in 1845.

Buckler visited Ludlow on 3 and 4 June 1822 and made 28 drawings, most of them of the Castle and Church but also one of the *Feathers* (see p.91). It is not known when Clayton came to Ludlow but it was probably some time before his work was published in *Timber Framed Edifices of the West Midlands*, published in 1846.

*Buckler's* South West View of Ludlow Church *shows the hexagonal porch, which was built in the early 14th century in the Decorated style of architecture. In plan and style the porch is similar to that at St Mary Redcliffe, Bristol, but it is not certain which porch was the older. Bristol was an important outlet for Ludlow's cloth while wine and other exotic items were brought in through the port. Buckler shows the flowing tracery of the porch windows and the short, stepped buttresses, which contrast with the Perpendicular features of the tower and the west end. To the right can be seen the back premises of buildings opening onto King Street but the present tall backs of Nos. 1, 2 and 3 King Street are not yet built.*

*This drawing of No. 24 Bull Ring was an incidental feature of Clayton's lithograph of the front of the* Feathers *(see p.91) but after enlargement it is a pleasing and informative picture in its own right, the best which has survived of any Ludlow shop before the age of photography. Whereas all Buckler's Ludlow drawings include only the architecture, Clayton sometimes introduces human figures and these give his pictures added historical interest. The man inside the shop is probably William Ward Evans, who kept a butcher's shop here from the late 1830s until 1850, while the lady in the first floor window is perhaps Mrs. Evans. Next door can be seen part of another butcher's shop, that of Samuel Deyos, who rented Corporation fields at Gravel Hill, presumably to fatten his cattle.*

*In spite of these two shops being next door to each other the Ludlow butchers of this time were scattered all over the town, in contrast to earlier periods, when they congregated in one area, e.g. in the Shambles at the top of Mill Street in the 17th century.*

1. *D.N.B.*

George Griffiths (d.1883) was a corn merchant at Bewdley, the river port on the Severn some 20 miles east of Ludlow. He also wrote on many topics and was interested in social causes, especially the reform of endowed grammar schools. A contemporary described him as 'a man of versatile gifts', though admitting that 'his literary ventures swallowed up his business fortunes'.[1] He achieved notoriety by polling only one vote in a Parliamentary election—his own.

His best known book is *Going to Markets and Grammar Schools, 1830-70*, which contains a memorable description of a coach journey from Bewdley to Ludlow in 1837:

> *Finding my business increase I resolved to go to Ludlow market every Monday, on the mail coach, which arrived at the Wheat Sheaf Inn, Load Street, about six o'clock in the morning, on its journey from Birmingham . . .*
>
> *The journey to Ludlow was the pleasantest I ever travelled. The road through the 'Far Forest' . . . and thence all the way to Cleobury Mortimer, was up and down very steep hills . . . The coachman pulled up at the Talbot Inn and as the horses were being changed, the main street ( . . . the only one) was all alive; the shopkeepers came out to have a stare, the boys and ne'er-do-wells stood gaping at the passengers, and as the coach moved away sundry remarks were loudly proclaimed, not very complimentary to our ears. Away we went up the street, the horses seeming to care very little for the load they drew . . . Away we flew, rising higher and higher . . . until we reached the top some six miles from Cleobury. Here was a sight worth travelling a hundred miles to see. We were on the top of the Clee Hill, 1200 feet above the valley and on a fine summer's morning the view . . . was very imposing. With the aid of a hand telescope, the whole of the country as far as Bristol was visible on the left, whilst the valley of the Corve on the right, and the hills of Radnorshire in front, made up an enchanting scene . . . When I was a boy in Birmingham I used to think that a stage coachman was the finest fellow in the world; his long whip, many-coloured coat, huge hat, top-boots, his four splendid horses, and the clean, well painted coach under his command . . . made him appear . . . a far superior person to any other mortal living; but I never thought about such glorious scenes as we witnessed between Bewdley and Ludlow and the glass of home brewed at the road side inn, and as in the case of the mail coaches the aristocratic driving through the turnpikes without paying tolls . . .*

In Ludlow Griffiths breakfasted at the *Rose and Crown* in Church Street on 'coffee and fish and toast of first class quality'. He wrote at length about the Castle and other antiquities but has little to say about the market itself except that the farmers 'were of a better sort than most, particularly those from Corve-Dale'. He dined at the *Elephant and Castle* where 'such a fine healthy set of tenants of the soil were seldom to be met with as at that table' though 'they grumbled a bit at something or other—either prices were too low, although the harvest was abundant, or the yield was too short, although the price was high'.

The Elephant and Castle Inn, *No.15 Bull Ring, a timber-framed building erected c.1662 though later rendered with stucco. Demolished in 1924 to make way for what is now the National Westminster Bank.*

1. Wedley, I.L., *Bewdley and its Surroundings* (1914), p.23.

# THOMAS WRIGHT, SENIOR, 1822,
# AND THOMAS WRIGHT, JUNIOR, 1841-43

Thomas Wright, senior, was a journeyman printer who came to Ludlow from Bradford in the 1790s as an employee of the bookseller and publisher, George Nicholson.[1] He was later employed by Henry Proctor (see p. 83) at No. 10 Broad Street. Before coming to Ludlow Wright had failed in a business enterprise of his own and was always in poor circumstances but he was a man of considerable learning and was interested in local history. In 1822 he wrote *The History and Antiquities of the Town of Ludlow and Descriptive and Historical Accounts of Gentlemens' Seats*, which was published by Proctor and Jones and which ran to a second edition in 1826. The format is small (4in. x 6½in.) but the book has 274 pages, 200 of which are devoted to Ludlow. One of the most original sections is that on customs, which contains a description of rope pulling on Shrove Tuesday:[2]

*Among the customs peculiar to this town, that of Rope Pulling is not the least extraordinary. On Shrove Tuesday the Corporation provide a Rope three inches in circumference and in length thirty-six yards, which is given out at one of the windows of the Market House as the clock strikes four: when a large body of the inhabitants divided into two parties, one contending for Castle Street and Broad Street Wards, and the other for Old Street and Corve Street Wards, commence an arduous struggle; and as soon as either party gains the victory by pulling the Rope beyond the prescribed limits, the pulling ceases; which is however renewed by a second, and sometimes by a third contest, the Rope being purchased by subscription from the victorious party and given out again ...*[3]

Thomas Wright, junior (1810-77), was brought up in Ludlow and attended the grammar school. 'His zeal for literary research showed itself in early youth'; but as the son of a poor man he would have had no chance of a university education had not a 'well-to-do neighbour', John Hutchins of No. 31 Broad Street, 'defrayed the expenses of his education at Cambridge'.[4] As an undergraduate he wrote a voluminous *History and Topography of Essex* and in later life he earned his living as a professional antiquary, writing many articles and over 100 books. These include edited transcriptions of many historical and literary records. Much of his work 'was hastily executed and errors abound' but 'his enthusiasm and industry were inexhaustible'.

*One of several small illustrations made from wooden blocks which were used in Thomas Wright's book and in his son's* History of Ludlow. *It shows the Borough arms over the entrance to Hosier's Almshouses in College Street. The arms consist of the lion of Mortimer and three white Yorkist roses, topped by the ostrich feathers of the Prince of Wales.*

Wright junior's greatest contribution to the history of Ludlow was *Churchwardens' Accounts of the Town of Ludlow ... from 1540 to the end of the Reign of Queen Elizabeth*, though after 1577 his transcription is selective. This was published in 1867 by the Camden Society of which he had been a founder member in 1838 and the first honorary secretary. He is better known locally for his *History of Ludlow and Neighbourhood*, which was published in two parts by Richard Jones in 1841 and 1843 and in one volume in 1852. As implied by the sub-title, 'A Popular Sketch of the History of the Welsh Border', this book of 541 pages is much more than a history of Ludlow, but it did include important material which had not been previously published, e.g. documents concerning the dissolution of Ludlow's religious houses in the mid-16th century and a fine inventory of the Castle taken in 1650.

1. Wright, 1867, p.148.
2. pp.193-4.
3. Burne, pp.319-21. A description given in 1884 is quoted: 'Lawyers and their clerks, tradesmen, gentlemen, and even parsons were there to give a push if not a pull, and a queer-looking set up they were when it was all over—all rags and tatters. The shops were shut at four o'clock, when the rope ... was given out of the Market Hall window by the Mayor ... if the struggle was carried down Mill Street, the Red Knob had won, and they dipped the knobs in the River Teme ... If the contest was carried into the Bull Ring, the Blue Knob was the victor ... Disorderly scenes, and the dangerous accidents which often happened ... caused it to be discontinued in 1851 ...'
4. *D.N.B.*

Anna Maria Fay and her niece Katherine came from Boston, U.S.A. They were distant relatives of the Salweys and in 1851-2 stayed at The Moor, Richard's Castle, two miles south of Ludlow. Their letters home were printed as *Victorian Days in England* (Boston, 1923). Many of their comments on Ludlow were about St Laurence's Parish Church, e.g. on Sunday, 9 November 1851, Anna Maria wrote to her mother:

*nothing could exceed the solemnity of the scene: the antique roof, the vaulted arches above us . . . the noble organ, the rich screens . . . the devout poor seated on the benches in the middle aisle . . . Around the gallery are blackboards framed in gilt, upon which are painted in yellow letters bequests from various individuals, among them that twelve of the poorest in the parish are to receive on every Sunday a loaf of bread, and outside the door in the vestibule are the loaves ranged along, while the beadle waits to distribute them . . .* [1]

Fine though the building was Anna Maria found much to criticise:

*The Te Deum was chanted to a rather ordinary double chant . . . while the words of the Jubilate and the Gloria were miserably divided, some gabbled and others drawled out . . .*

She was even more censorious of the Rector:

*Mr. Phillips, the rector, is a miserably low churchman—indeed they say he is a very bad man, and his face just-ifies the report.*[2] *He is so unpopular that the Dissenting chapels and the alehouses are filled on Sundays . . .*[3]

Not surprisingly, the procession of the Mayor, aldermen and councillors attracted her attention:

*Immediately under the pulpit are four pews lined with red, in which sit the Mayor and Corporation in blue silk gowns trimmed with fur, to which the former adds a red collar. They read the service out of great red books about eighteen inches long, and as they marched out of the church in procession two officials preceded them carrying silver maces.*[4]

On Sunday 16 November Anna Maria wrote another letter:

*'We have just returned from church at Ludlow where Aunt Catherine* [Salwey] *has to perform quite an important office. It is customary that, when a new Mayor is elected, on the first Sunday after the election the Archdeacon of Salop preaches a sermon in aid of the Charity Schools, and the collection is taken up at the door, on which occasion it is the etiquette to ask two ladies to hold the plates . . . the money was counted in the vestry-room . . . (and) . . . amounted to £33 13s . . .*

Thirteen years later Katherine Fay again visited St Laurence's on a second visit to The Moor. In a letter to her aunt she describes the 1859-60 restoration, carried out to the design of G.G. Scott, later Sir Gilbert Scott, the major re-storer of the period:

*It would do your heart good to see it. Without being made new-looking, it has been restored as nearly as possible to its original condition. The whitewash has been scraped away, the galleries removed, the pews lowered, the organ taken away from between the chancel and the nave, and, in fact, every attraction that good taste combined with veneration for antiquity could suggest.*

---

1. One of the charities endowed by Thomas Lane (d.1676); the money came from property west of Frog Lane (now St John's Lane).
2. John Phillips (1795-1867), from Pontesbury near Shrewsbury, was Rector of Ludlow, 1841-67.
3. The Ecclesiastical Census (PRO:HO 129/352) made on 30 March 1851 confirms that the nonconformist churches in Ludlow were attracting large congregations, though the return for St Laurence's, made by Phillips, was ambiguous.
4. Maces, symbolising authority, were carried to church in front of the Corporation since the 16th century or earlier, just as the reg-alia of trade guilds preceded their members. The Great Mace, carried by the Common Serjeant, and the smaller maces, carried by the Mace Bearer, all date from the second half of the 17th century.

*This print of the interior of St Laurence's was made by Edward Hodson the Younger, son of Edward Hodson, book-seller, who traded at what is now No. 59 Broad Street between 1820 and 1835. It shows clearly many of the features mentioned by Anna Maria Fay though their appearance has often been enhanced for artistic effect. The light streaming through a clerestory window on the north side of the Church is presumably an interesting artist's error.*

*This photograph by Thomas Jones (see pp.110-1) was taken soon after the 1859-60 restoration, and shows the Church much as it was seen by Katherine Fay in 1864. The contrast with Hodson's print is striking. The uniform low oak pews accentuate the delicacy and grace of the nave arcades while the tower arch soars upward uncluttered by the organ and its gallery. The glow of light under the crossing comes from the now revealed lantern. The view eastwards to the high altar is characteristic of mid-19th century church restoration, as urged by the Cambridge Camden Society.*

Walter White (1811-93) was a well-known writer of travel books, one of which, *All Round the Wrekin* (1860), gives original and often amusing comments on mid-Victorian Ludlow.[1] He began his working life as a cabinet maker but then became a clerk and was later Librarian to the Royal Society. Most of his books were based on walking holidays, such as that of 1860, when he walked in Shropshire, spending a day in Ludlow during a July heatwave.

After a night at the *Feathers*, 'the most picturesque hotel in the county' he began with a walk on Whitcliffe:

*Whitcliff is one of the sides of a defile alike high and precipitious, through which flows the Teme . . . The front of the precipice is rough, and deeply excavated here and there by quarries, while its brow is decorated with fern and foxglove, gorse, thyme and dandelion, as if to multiply pleasures for those who recline thereon . . .*

He proceeded to the Castle, noting on the way the Russian cannon which Ludlow Borough Council had purchased from the War Department two years previously:

*The main entrance (to the castle) is . . . an arched gateway . . . which gains nothing in picturesque effect by having in front of it one of those stupid trophies from Sebastopol—a Russian gun. It seems to me a mistake to have distributed those ugly things over the land; eyesores in the quiet streets of country towns . . . The Greeks, as I have read, used to set up wooden trophies, so that the memory of quarrels should not be too long perpetuated . . .*

*'The River Teme, Castle Hill and Whitcliffe', one of a series of 'picturesque views of Ludlow and district' published in the early 20th century by J.C. Austen, bookseller and printer at No.59 Broad Street. The scene is little changed from that described by Walter White some 50 years earlier. Whitcliffe, on the left, has less vegetation than today. The weir which provided water power for the mills of Mill Street can be seen in the foreground and to the left are some of the bare rocks exposed by ancient quarrying.*

1. The Ludlow account occupies pp.81-92.

*The street market in Castle Square, photographed in the 1870s. The man in the foreground is wearing a hat of the kind described by White. Details of the old Market Hall (demolished in 1887) can be seen on the right. One of the town's finest Georgian houses, built about 1775, can be seen beyond the square. From 1867-1908 this was the Rectory, the home of the Rev. E. ff. Clayton, whose wife was a member of the Clive family of Oakly Park.*

After touring the Castle, White gives a unique glimpse of the street market which was still held in Castle Square:

*The contrast was great between the quiet of the castle and the noisy market-place, where, when I came forth, business was at high tide. What numbers of rustics were crowding hither and thither, clad in fustian and wearing a black hat with hemispherical crown and broad brim, followed by smock-fronted boys. How they grinned at the staring placards of an itinerant circus; and how strange their talk sounded to unaccustomed ears. 'Did ya ha' the starm isterd'y?' - 'How bin ya?' - 'Don't ya meddle wi' them there ducks.' - 'Well, I beant a gween to.' - 'Be you a gween hoam a'ter markut?' - 'I think I shan.' - 'Na, I binna.' Prominent among the commodities offered for sale were yeast and poultry—and great was the chaffering for 'barm and birds'. It was pitiable to see squadrons of ducks, with legs bound, sitting on the hot stones, and cocks and hens crammed into coops, all gasping incessantly with the heat, for the thermometer marked 90°.*

*'Moine bangs yourn' said one red-cheeked woman to her neighbours at the next stand. 'Ah, but moine'll be sold fust' was the answer in the somewhat shrill tone which seems to be a characteristic of the women here, as it is of the sex in Wales.*

Walter White next went to the Parish Church, which was being 'restored', to the design of Gilbert Scott. He describes the 'labourers, masons, carpenters, glaziers, and sculptors, swarming at the work of restoration' and continues:

*Notwithstanding the confusion, the scaffoldings round some of the columns, and the entire removal of the floor, the sight of the six pointed arches springing high aloft on each side of the nave, of the four mighty arches of the tower, and of the handsome lantern above, was so gratifying to the eye that to tarry awhile seemed the happiest way of improving the time . . .*

John Evans (1814-76) was a Ludlow bookseller who opened a business at the Assembly Rooms in Castle Street in 1849. In 1861 he published a 92 page *Hand-Book to Ludlow* which contains 56 information-packed pages on the town itself and also 14 walks and eight rides into the surrounding countryside. Evans was a deacon of the Ludlow Congregational Church and his *Hand-Book* includes a three and a half page section headed 'Dissenting Chapels and Sunday Schools'. There had been a small group of Independents in Ludlow since the late 17th century. Evans relates the events which led to the foundation of their chapel:

> *The persecution of this small body of inoffensive people seems to have been brought to a crisis in the early part of the last century . . . on Sunday, March 21, 1731, somewhat more than twenty persons met together in the house of Mrs. Jones, in High Street . . . for the purpose, as they had been wont, of religious worship. They had scarcely commenced, however, when a mob collected, who furiously attacked the house, throwing stones through the windows, to the great terror and danger of the persons within, on which Mrs. Jones, Peter Griffin and James Wynde[1] went to the high bailiff, Mr. Henry Davies, to request his assistance; but he, instead of helping, charged them with the riot, . . . notwithstanding Mrs. Jones and her friends produced a licence . . . The mob hearing how matters stood, returned to the charge, and broke every window in the house . . .*

The Ludlow Independents were fined but their case was taken up by the London Committee of Protestant Dissenting Ministers and eventually the Ludlow magistrates had to make compensation. Evans relates how the incident prompted them to build their own chapel:

> *They were driven by persecution to seek quietude for their religious worship to a retired and secluded spot, at the bottom of Corve Street, adjoining the River Corve, in the year 1731 . . . the chapel was built by much effort among themselves and a few sympathising friends from other parts; and so desirous were these poor people of having a place of their own, that the women aided in the work, by carrying stones for the building in their aprons.[2]*

The unusual photograph below shows the timber-frame of No.16 High Street, the house where the 1731 riot occurred. It was a Corporation property leased in the early 18th century to Mrs. Jones, widow, and her son, Philip Jones,

a mercer. The frame itself has been much altered but the upper horizontal member is probably the wallplate of the house inhabited by the Joneses. Like other High Street properties it was refronted and raised, probably in the early 19th century, when timber framed buildings were unfashionable and when the town's increasing population required more living space.

The photograph was taken soon after 1900, when both No.16 and No.17 (on the left) were owned by E.W. and W. Philips, who wished to standardise their fronts. The previous plain stuccoed front of No.16 (see photograph on p. 105) was replaced by one that matched that of No.17.

No.15, on the right, was occupied by Edwin Sanders when the photograph was taken but until 1900 had been the grocer's shop of Edmund Jones. Like other Ludlow properties its attic storey was lit by a semicircular window.

1. These were the leaders of the church. Peter Griffin was a dyer in Corve Street and James Wynde a tailor in Castle ward.
2. The chapel was situated close to the River Corve near the bottom of Corve Street and was at the back of a property, some 60ft. from the street. It remained in regular use until 1830 when a new Congregational Chapel was built in Old Street but was used for occasional services until the 1930s. An internal photograph taken in 1910 shows the 18th-century box pews and pulpit. It was demolished c.1960.

# The Ludlow Advertiser,

PRINTED AND PUBLISHED BY JOHN CROSSE, EVERY SATURDAY MORNING, AT HIS GENERAL PRINTING OFFICE, 18, KING STREET, LUDLOW.

| No. 226. | SATURDAY, JANUARY 24, 1863. | PRICE THREE-HALF-PENCE |
|---|---|---|

The Ludlow Advertiser was founded in September 1858 by John Crosse, the bookseller and printer who had taken over William Felton's business at No.18 King Street. The 'tiser, issued weekly ever since, has had its fair share of journalistic oddities and foibles and someone wanting a quick laugh from a Ludlow audience might be tempted to remark that Crosse has a lot to answer for, particularly as he replaced the timber framed premises he acquired by what is commonly regarded as one of the worst of Ludlow's late Victorian buildings. More seriously, the paper has been a well-loved feature of local life, not least because of the contributions of its correspondents. The following specimen is not only amusing but contains useful historical information. It is from the first page of the issue of 25 October 1862.

*Sir, Very few of your Ludlow readers are unaware of . . . the risk of personal injury which every inhabitant of the town runs while walking along the streets about seven o'clock in the evening . . . The reason for this is that the drapers closing their shops at seven p.m. keep their shutters in most cases up a narrow entry and, whether it is that their young men have a taste for racing or that they are simply enjoyed at the end of their day's work, it is certain that shutters and iron bars dart about in such numbers and with such velocity as to take away one's breath . . . Unfortunately this is not all. A shutter propelled against one's cheek or an iron bar planted in the ribs are trifling perils compared with another which menaces passers by—Those shopkeepers who have no passages keep their shutters in their cellars and pass them up between rollers through a narrow slit in the pavement. They are not pushed up softly but spring from below with noise and velocity of a rocket. Now, conceive, Sir, a respectable, short, stout gentleman—there are several such in Ludlow—with thick gloves on, peaceful looking, and a cotton umbrella under his arm walking along High Street, to such an individual one of these slits would be as terrible as a mine. A vigorously propelled shutter, well applied, would hoist our friend as neatly as a barrel of gunpowder.*

A photograph of High Street c.1895, looking west towards the recently opened Town Hall. The raised awnings on the south facing side of the street suggest it is the middle of the day but the shops seem to be attracting little custom.

High Street is the widest and most important of the streets between the 'rows' of 'selda' which colonised the wide market place in the 13th century. Each 'selda' then occupied 'a third burgage' and though some properties have amalgamated the pattern of small shops persists. The row on the left was once 'Lockiers' Row' and that on the right 'Shoe-makers' Row', but by the 19th century the trades had diversified.

In 1895 there were 17 shops in the High Street, 10 of which sold clothes or footwear. One of these was E.W. and W. Philips, tailors, whose premises can be seen on the corner. Victorian shop windows with small panes can be seen, while further up the street some shops display their wares externally.

The development of photography in the middle years of the 19th century provides a new and rich source of information for the visual historian. Photography became a new profession and early practitioners toured the country, taking large numbers of pictures and selling the prints for profit. One of the best was Francis Bedford (1816-94), who achieved celebrity when he accompanied the Prince of Wales to India in 1862.[1] Bedford was the first photographer of national standing known to have worked in Ludlow and a number of his prints have survived, some of them in private collections. They can be dated in the early 1860s. They were taken with an instantaneous stereoscopic camera and appeared initially as stereoscopic pairs mounted on bright yellow cards.

Several of Bedford's photographs are street scenes, which feature strong perspectives, often with vehicles in the foreground to provide interest for the viewer. Others are of the Castle, a popular subject for the early photographers, though Bedford's views are often from unusual angles.

This is a rare view of the middle of Corve Street looking south towards the Parish Church. On the far right is No.32, the pleasant three-bay Georgian house owned and occupied by Peter Klein, one of the authors of this book, and his family. Next door are Nos.31 and 30a, at this time an old glover's workshop and adjoining cottage; these were demolished in 1902 to make way for Corve Villas. The five-bay Georgian house beyond was built c.1750 for John Hosier, a master glover. Further up the street a jettied timber framed building can be seen, on the site of the present entrance to Castle Garage. To the left, No.114 still has its walled garden, later partially built upon, while beyond is the gable end of a building on the north corner of Station Drive which had disappeared by the 1880s.

This is an eastwards view from the curtain wall of the Castle. In the foreground are the ruins of the Great Kitchen, built at the same time as the Hall in the late 13th century. The large mullioned and transomed window had no glass but is rebated for shutters. Typically, parts of the walls are smothered in vegetation. Beyond is the round chapel of St Mary Magdalene, built in the early 12th century, and the eastern wall of the inner bailey.

1. *D.N.B.*

These two photographs provide a fine picture of the Butter Cross and of the eastern side of upper Broad Street in the 1860s. The 'piazza' or covered way, which was given its present appearance by the street commissioners in the 1790s, gives this part of the town its distinctive character. Nearly all the timber-framed buildings have plastered facades, including No.2 Broad Street (on the right of the left hand photograph); this building was 'restored' in 1871, but recent repairs have revealed that this was done by applying ornately carved pine blacked to simulate oak. This was 'Butchers' Row' in the 18th century but by 1861 there was only one butcher, alongside three grocers,

one confectioner, one boot and shoe dealer, one dealer of glass and china, one tailor and one bookseller. The four-wheeled vehicle outside the *Angel* is the hotel 'bus' used to convey guests from the station. In 1861 there were 60 residents in the 11 houses fronting this part of Broad Street, including 16 sleeping-in servants, a contrast with the seven residents of 1979, when most of the upper floors were used as store-rooms (both sets of figures ignore guests at the *Angel*).

The view to the right is from inside the round chapel, looking east through the chancel arch. Victorian tourists lounge on the foundations of the former rectangular chancel. Parts of the wall arcade can be seen on either side of the chapel. The chancel arch, with its three orders of columns and arches, is a most impressive feature and in places is lavishly decorated, e.g. the front and soffit (underside) of the innermost arch is diapered with stars.

Louise Rayner (1829-1924) was born in Derby, one of a family of painters. She became a popular topographical artist, living largely from the sale of her paintings. She specialised in watercolours, especially of old cathedral cities and market towns. 'Her architectural drawing' is held to be 'remarkably accurate', though many of her street scenes 'display varying degrees of idealisation'.[1] She painted three known watercolours of Ludlow, probably on a single visit in the 1870s. Two of these are reproduced below.[2]

*This watercolour of Castle Street was discovered in a shop window in Stratford in 1976 and bought by the Friends of Ludlow Museum. The busy street market is a characteristic Rayner scene. She has included several of the carriers.' carts and vans which were used on regular services to and from the surrounding villages. The old Market Hall (see p. 79) dominates the centre of the picture. To the right, between High Street and Market Street, can be seen the premises of James and Edward Harding, once the George Inn. The 19th century George Inn, a favourite rendezvous of the carriers, can be seen on the left, with its large painted sign board partly hidden by trees inside the railed garden of No.14.*

*This picture of the Bull Ring, looking south, shows another busy part of the town, called 'the Beaste Market' in the 17th century. In the centre is the Tolsey, a 15th-century timber framed building, once open on the ground floor, with a court room above. By the 19th century the building was smothered in plaster, there was a small extension to the west and the ground floor was occupied by two small shops: John Anthony, hairdresser, on the left, and Samuel Cox, gardener and seed merchant, on the right. Beyond can be seen the tall facades of Nos.43 and 44, the premises of Dawes and Bowen, wine and spirit merchants. The picture is full of human interest and children play freely in the middle of the street.*

1. Gillison, M., *Louise Rayner, 1829-1924* (Grosvenor Museum, Chester, 1978), p.5.
2. The third painting, of the Butter Cross, is in Ludlow Museum.

# BENJAMIN STONE,
# 1880s AND 1890s

Benjamin Stone (1838-1914) was a Birmingham businessman who became the first Mayor of Sutton Coldfield in 1886 and was later knighted for political services.[1] He was a dedicated amateur photographer and took more than 22,000 prints, most of them from 1888 onwards. The collection, now lodged at Birmingham Public Reference Library, has 32 Ludlow prints, three of which are reproduced below. Stone was more concerned with historical record than with 'artistic creations' and as these pictures show he liked to work when there were few people about; but he was well regarded in his lifetime and in 1911 he was the official photographer at the coronation of George V.

*This picture of Broad Street was taken in the early 1880s. The eastern side of the street is recorded more often than the western because artists and photographers alike wanted to include the church tower as a picturesque background.*

*As in previous centuries this central part of Broad Street was a fashionable residential area. The house on the far right, No.28, was Miss Fanny Brown's 'private school for boys', one of several such establishments in the town.*

*The facades of most of the houses have changed little in the last century but No.22, above Brand Lane, is much altered while the pleasing six-bay house directly in line with the church tower was replaced in 1879 by 'the pretentious imitation-Tudor of Lloyds Bank' (Pevsner).*

*This photograph shows the Feathers in the early 1890s. It then rivalled the Angel as the town's leading hotel and important local functions were held there, e.g. a Military Ball of the Shropshire Yeomanry in 1889; while 'Post and Saddle Horses' as well as 'Flys, Broughams, Brakes and Private Omnibuses' were hired from the adjoining mews. It also continued to serve as a local inn and farmers' luncheons were served on market days.*

*The ornate timber framed facade was now much admired, e.g. in 1894 the writer of a travel book claimed: 'The picturesque Feathers is perhaps as fine an example of a black and white timbered building as may be found anywhere'. The photograph shows that all three front gables now have pierced bargeboards with geometrical patterns while the simulated cusped panels covering some of the second floor window panes are still in position, though they were removed in the 'restoration' of 1898.*

*This beautiful photograph, taken in 1888, is the earliest yet found of the James I Lounge, then used as the hotel dining room. This room was the Great Chamber of the early 17th century home of Rees Jones, an attorney at the Council of the Marches, and is the most lavishly decorated room in Ludlow. The plain panelling focuses attention on the elaborate over-mantle which contains the arms of James I, who united the crowns of England and Scotland. Decorplasterwork still covers all but the central part of the ceiling and its intertwining roses and thistles, symbolising the two countries, can be seen in among the star-shaped strapwork. Tendrils of vines, suggesting luxury and botanical exuberance, can be seen on the spine beams.*

1. Leaflet in Birmingham Public Library, *The Stone Collection of Photographs.*

Thomas Jones (1837-c.1905) is the first professional photographer known to have taken up residence in Ludlow; before this the town had been served by travelling photographers who advertised their presence in the local press. Jones was born at Eccleshall in Staffordshire and set up business with his father Robert Jones at No. 51 Broad Street about 1857, when he was a young man of 20.[1] In 1861 Robert moved to Leominster, leaving Thomas on his own, though assisted by his sister Jane, who was a photographer in her own right.

Jones was to dominate the trade in the town for the rest of the century, though a branch opened at Hereford in 1869 was not a success.[2] By 1895 he was in partnership with his son and by 1900 also with Walter Harper. Harper was sole proprietor from 1913 until his death in 1932, when the studio was closed.

Photographs taken by Jones survive in many places. He took portraits of groups and individuals and these are to be found in private collections.[3] There is also a series of small carte-de-visite photographs taken during the 1860s. These were gummed to a card mount but could also be purchased as unmounted prints for sticking in scrap albums.

Jones took all the well-known Ludlow 'sights'—the Castle, the Church, the *Feathers*—but being a Ludlovian by adoption he could afford time to look for unusual views and for seasonal effects. As reflected in this small selection, he had a particular fondness for the River Teme and catches it in changing moods.

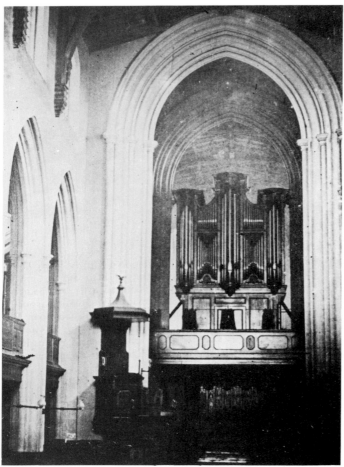

This remarkable photograph, printed from a glass plate negative, is the earliest dateable photograph attributable to Thomas Jones. It shows the interior of the Parish Church before the 1859-60 restoration and must have been taken before February 1859 when the organ builders Messrs. Gray and Davison removed the Snetzler organ prior to the demolition of the old organ-gallery. specially built in 1764. The splendid three-decker pulpit and details of the galleries, the gas-lighting system and the box pews can be seen.

A hot summer's day on Whitcliffe, taken from near the *Ludlow Arms*. There is a distant view of the Church tower between the two large horse-chestnut trees; the pinnacles are missing from the top of the tower, indicating a date between 1884 and 1890. A horse drawn waggon labours up the steep track on the left while the sleepy sheep rest in the cool beneath the branches.

1. Census returns and trade directories; *Ludlow Advertiser*, 4 January 1862, p.2.
2. The branch was at No. 18 King Street, with Jane Jones as manageress. Unfortunately it was next door to the well-established studio of Ladmore's and by 1876 John Thirlwall had succeeded to the business.
3. E.g. the album now in the Shropshire County Library.

This photograph is dated January 1881 and shows nearly 200 people enjoying themselves on ice, the picture being taken from Castle Walk. The scene is reminiscent of the Flemish painter Peter Brueghel and prophetic of the 20th-century landscapes of Lowry. The River Teme became quite thickly frozen during a series of very harsh winters at the end of the 19th century. On the far bank can be seen the fields bordering Halton Lane, most of which had been enclosed by hedges since the 16th century, while on the town side of the river is Castle Meadow, divided by 19th-century wooden fences.

A leisurely spring scene on the River Teme north west of the Castle. Like the view from Whitcliffe, this was taken between 1884 and 1889. Boating for pleasure on the river was introduced as a municipal amenity in the early 1880s. On the right is a gravel and mud bank known as Batty's island, which is now the authorized limit for rowing boats. The land on the right is part of the Oakly Park estate and the hedged track from Halton Lane can be seen on a low terrace, just in front of the trees.

A Jones 'carte', showing the prospect from Whitcliffe looking east towards Ludford Bridge. The weir and the shallows below it can be clearly seen at the end of Mill Street, and also the mill which was swept away by the great flood of 1886. Whitcliffe at this time was much more open than today and fine views abounded. Its closely-cropped appearance was largely due to grazing sheep which kept the vegetation under control. On the right can be seen the quarries of Silurian limestone from which much of the town's building stone was taken.

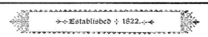

**⋅÷ Established ÷ 1822.⋅÷⋅**

# ROBERT HENRY HODGES,

(Late CHAPLIN HODGES,)

## Iron & Brass Founder,

### MILLWRIGHT

AND

### AGRICULTURAL IMPLEMENT MAKER,

## CASTLE FOUNDRY, LUDLOW.

ooooooooooooooooooooooooooooooo

*Every description of Castings Made to Order.*

IRON WATER WHEELS, Over-Shot, Breast-Shot or Under-Shot.

IRON SLUICE BOLTS and FRAMES for WATER WAYS, and FITTED.

CAST and WROUGHT IRON SHAFTING.

PLUMBER BLOCKS and COUPLINGS, BEVEL, SPUR and MORTICE WHEELS, PULLEYS and all kinds of GEARING for STEAM, WATER or HORSE POWER.

ENGINE BARS, FLUE BARS, DOORS, FRAMES and GRATES, for OVENS or FURNACES.

PUMPS, all Sizes and Depths, to Order.

PALISADES and TOMB RAILINGS to Order.

GRAVE MARKERS, all Sizes, to Order.

CELLAR DOORS and FRAMES, and Fitted.

TRUCK, DRILL and PLOUGH WHEELS, and all kinds of PLOUGH CASTINGS.

DRAINAGE PIPES, GRATES, WELL COVERS and all kinds of CASTINGS for DRAINAGE WORK Made to Order.

AGRICULTURAL IMPLEMENTS Repaired on the Shortest Notice.

☞ ESTIMATES GIVEN IF REQUIRED. ☜

The art of advertising came of age in the late 19th century and advertisements often give a great deal of useful information which is hard to come by from other sources. Photographs taken from the 1880s show bills pasted on boards and other available surfaces and many small items survive in trade directories, newspapers and periodicals.

The trade advertisement printed here, from Porter's *Directory of Shropshire* (1888), shows a long list of products of the Hodges iron-foundry at Castle Mill, Dinham. Cast-iron, in the 19th century, seemed to be the infinitely versatile material that could be made into almost anything; it was also ideal for industry on a small local scale where tailor-made components in small numbers were required. The Castle Foundry was the nearest thing to heavy industry in Ludlow, their products including water-wheels, cast and wrought-iron shafting, pulleys and gears; indeed their principal trade was as millwrights which they had followed since the establishment of the firm, then Chaplin Hodges, in Lower Broad Street in 1822. The move to Castle Mill was made shortly before 1839 and the business thrived until 1890 when it was taken over by their foundry manager, William John Roberts, who moved it to his new Phoenix Works in Gravel Hill.

Much of the foundry's bread-and-butter work consisted of small iron castings such as ovens, grates, pumps and drain covers. Included in this list were cellar doors which today are perhaps still the most obvious examples of their surviving work. There are at least a dozen specimens in the Ludlow streets, most bearing a date between 1841 and 1881, the earliest with a latticed decoration distinctively inscribed 'HODGES LUDLOW FOUNDREY'. Later examples are covered in a flower pattern which combined ornament with an effective non-slip surface.

The photograph below shows the cellar cover of No. 145 Corve Street, the earliest with a flower pattern. The inscription shows that it was made in 1846, just after the house had been bought by Francis Massey, a wine merchant in business at No. 46 Bull Ring.

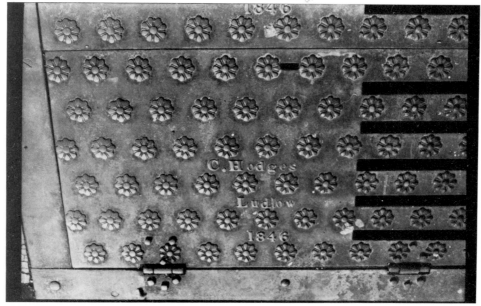

Oliver Baker (1856-1939) was the son of a Birmingham artist. He soon developed his own artistic and antiquarian interests and whilst still a young man made the acquaintance of the Ludlow bookseller, George Woolley, who had been in business at No.2 Bull Ring since 1863. Like other booksellers before him Woolley saw that there was profit to be made from local guidebooks and between 1884 and 1924 Woolley's *Ludlow Guide* ran to many editions. The substance of that guide had been written by Thomas Wright (see p.99) but in the early 1880s Woolley employed Baker to write additional sections. It was then that Baker was urged to write a more ambitious work called *Ludlow: Town and Neighbourhood*, which was first published in 1888, though there were other editions in 1889 and 1906.

Baker had a freshness of style which rendered his work easily readable. He noticed buildings which were often ignored, e.g. 'the ruined tower at the back of the *Feathers*, placed so as to strengthen the wall on this side where the natural defences were weakest'; and he is one of the first writers to refer to houses outside the popular tourist area, e.g. 'at the lower end of Corve Street'.[1] The book includes '67 special sketches' which, George Woolley claimed in his preface, 'have been reproduced in fac-simíle by the eminent process-engravers, the Typographic Etching Company of London'. The sketches are pleasing though slightly romanticised.

The sketch to the right shows Harp Lane, one of the town's narrowest streets, between the old Butchers' Row on the left and the old Shoemakers' Row on the right, two of the lines of shops which colonised the original market place. The central gutter and the jettied buildings on the right give the street an historic atmosphere.

The sketch (below right) of the yard of the *Bull Inn* is typical of Baker's style. The long range on the right was built in the late Middle Ages and has a deep jetty with particularly heavy joists. The gable building at the end of the yard, over the entrance from the Bull Ring, was a 17th-century extension. On the left are back buildings behind the *Elephant and Castle* (see p.98), which were cleared away when the inn was demolished in 1924.

Oliver Baker became a well-known figure in artistic circles in Birmingham. He later moved to Stratford-on-Avon, where he wrote his best known work, *In Shakespeare's Warwickshire*, which was published in 1937, two years before his death.

1. The old tower is actually part of No.27 the Bull Ring, a little further up the street than the *Feathers*.

*54 Broad Street, the boyhood home of the Weyman brothers. The house was built c.1770.*

Henry Weyman (1851-1941) was born in Ludlow, the eldest son of a Broad Street solicitor. He lived there all his life, except when a school-boy at Shrewsbury and an undergraduate at Oxford. He became a part-ner in the family firm but found ample time both for public service—he was Mayor of Ludlow three times—and for historical research, particu-larly into the history of Ludlow, for which he had great affection. He published a number of long papers for the *Transactions of the Shropshire Archaeological Society*, founded in 1878, while his *Ludlow in Bye-Gone Days* (1913) is still the best book available on the life and topography of historic Ludlow. His scholarly, painstaking research is in the best tradition of local history and later workers have paid tribute to 'the sterling work of this local antiquary'.[1]

The chapter on 'The Weeping Cross' in *Ludlow in Bye-Gone Days* (pp.40-1) can be used to illustrate Weyman's technique as a local hist-orian. The cross stood on the river side of what is now the junction of Weeping Cross Lane with Temeside and is marked as an antiquity on O.S. maps (SO 51707432). The remnants of a small mound can still be detected on the site.

Weyman begins with a general discussion of weeping crosses and their functions:

*There are not many Weeping Crosses in England . . . (they) are said to have been originally erected as the place for the performance of expiatory rites by those who were compelled to do penance . . . To this cross the weeping penitent was conducted to confess his sins to the Priest . . . The Oswestry Cross of Wailing is said to have been erected at the time of . . . plague . . . as the place where . . . Country people could bring their produce to the outskirts of the town with-out running the risk of infection . . .*

Weyman continues with a reference to a 15th-century deed in the collection known as 'Ancient Deeds' in the Public Record Office. He was the first Ludlovian after Wright to systematically explore the national archives and made many visits to London for the purpose.

*Grant by Margery Grymme, of Sheet, to Ralph Ashton, of that Corn Mill called Sheet Mill, with the fish work thereunto belonging, upon the River of Teme just by the Weeping Cross of Ludlow.* (Ancient Deeds, vol.3. 6109)

He goes on to quote from a presentment to the Borough Court in 1623. This was one of the voluminous records of Ludlow Corporation, now at the Shropshire County Record Office, but then housed in Ludlow. Weyman had the great advantage of unrestrained access to these records. He pointed out that as well as giving information on the weeping cross the entry shows that the custom of beating the bounds of the parish went back as far as the early 17th century:

*We present Robert Townshend for that he hath forfeited a pain of £2 for not making and maintaining a sufficient stile wicket and a bridge over the ditch which leadeth into the Friar Meadow near the Weeping Cross, being the ancient highway for the Parish of Ludlow to make their perambulation in Rogation week and being the common highway and ancient Church way to Ludford.*

He went on to identify Robert Townshend and all the places mentioned, pointing out, for instance, that 'the ancient Church Way' connected distant parts of Ludford parish. He thus fulfilled another requirement of the good local historian, that he should be able to relate his material both to other local events and to the local landscape.

1. Ganderton and Lafond, p.7

Stanley Weyman (1855-1928) was Henry's younger brother who trained as a barrister but had more success as a popular historical novelist. He established his reputation in the 1890s, first with *A Gentleman of France* (1893), then with *Under the Red Robe* (1896), which was dramatised at the Haymarket. From 1898 to 1928 he lived at Ruthin in North Wales where he is commemorated by a public statue.

The only novel where the setting is recognisably Ludlow is *The New Rector* (1891), Weyman's second work. Weyman was an admirer of Trollope but here neither plot nor characterisation are completely convincing. An absentee patron, Lord Dynmore, has appointed the young Reginald Lindo to the living of Claversham, mistaking him for his uncle, who had died the previous year. The theme of the novel is the relationship between the young incumbent and the Rev. Clode, the curate of Claversham who had cherished hopes of his own preferment.

Claversham is supposedly in Warwickshire but names and other details are freely borrowed from south Shropshire. The archdeacon, for example, lives at 'Kingsford Carbonel . . . among the orchards and hopyards'. There had been no new rector at Ludlow since the Rev. ff. Clayton was instituted in 1867, when Weyman was a 12-year-old schoolboy; and the hesitant Reginald Lindo is certainly not the formidable ffarington Clayton. But Weyman shows himself sensitive to small town church politics as he describes the speculations of the interregnum:

> *There was scarcely a person in Claversham who did not give some time . . . to the interesting question who was to be the new rector. The rector was a big factor in the town life. Girls wondered whether he would be young, and hoped he would dance. Their mothers were sanguine that he would be unmarried, and their fathers that he would play whist . . . And some trusted that he would let things be, and some hoped that he would cleanse the stables. And only one thing was certain and sure and immutably fixed—that, whoever he was, he would not be able to please everybody.*

The description of Lindo's arrival by train and his walk to the rectory would also have been familiar to Ludlow readers:

> *Lindo let his eyes travel up the wide steep street before him, until it rested on the noble tower which crowned the little hill and looked down now, as it had looked down for five centuries, on the red roofs clustering about it . . . Near the top of the street a quaint, narrow flight of steps conducted them to the churchyard—an airy, elevated place, surrounded on three sides by the church and houses, but open on the fourth, on which a terraced walk, running along the summit of the old town wall . . . afforded a wide view of plain and hill.*

*The medieval Rectory in College Street. This building is obviously the one Weyman had in mind but between 1841 and 1978 the rectors lived elsewhere in the town.*

*The rough-cast facade conceals a complex building with thick stone walls and medieval timber framing. Recent recording has shown that the central cross wing and the right hand range have collar-rafter roofs and may be the oldest surviving roof structure in Ludlow. The original passage through the cross-wing was very high, perhaps to accommodate carts bringing the tithes which were an important part of the rector's income.*

*The site of the medieval Linney Gate can be seen to the right. Beyond are modern houses in Linney.*

Alfred Edward Housman (1859-1936) was a brilliant if rather pedantic classical scholar, who became Professor of Latin, first at University College, London, then at Cambridge, in spite of failing his degree at Oxford. His personal life was rarely happy and at times tragic but he found solace in writing poetry. Much of this was pre-occupied with death and personal sorrow, yet he had an extraordinary gift for beautiful and exact phrases, which helped to give him popular appeal.

He was born in Worcestershire and spent his boyhood in Bromsgrove, developing 'a sentimental feeling for Shropshire because its hills were our western horizon'.[1] He took much of his imagery from the county, though admitting he 'did not know it well'. His first anthology of poems, published in 1896, was called *The Shropshire Lad*, because many of his thoughts were expressed through a young man who apparently lived in the county. He died in 1936 and his ashes were buried in Ludlow churchyard, just outside the north door.

Ludlow provided the setting for six of Housman's poems, two of which are reproduced and discussed below.[2]

*The Recruit*

*Leave your home behind, lad,*
*And reach your friends your hand,*
*And go, and luck go with you*
*While Ludlow tower shall stand.*

*Oh, come you home of Sunday,*
*When Ludlow streets are still,*
*And Ludlow bells are calling*
*To farm and lane and mill.*[3]

*Or come you home of Monday,*
*When Ludlow market hums*
*And Ludlow chimes are playing*
*'The conquering hero comes'.*

*Come you home a hero,*
*Or come not home at all,*
*The lads you leave will mind you*
*Till Ludlow tower shall fall.*

*And you will list the bugle*
*That blows in lands of morn,*
*And make the foes of England*
*Be sorry you were born.*

*And you till trump of doomsday*
*On lands of morn may lie,*
*And make the hearts of comrades*
*Be heavy where you lie.*

*Leave your home behind you,*
*Your friends by field and town;*
*Oh, town and field will mind you*
*Till Ludlow tower is down.*

'The Recruit', the third poem in *The Shropshire Lad*, was written in January 1895. The heroism of volunteering for battle had a romantic appeal to Housman and several of his poems are about soldiers. The second and third verses give memorable glimpses of Ludlow's changing moods but the real theme of the poem is man's struggle against the odds, which may bring a soldier back home a hero—or leave him in a foreign grave. Throughout, the tower of Ludlow parish church, the tallest and most imposing in Shropshire, is a symbol of permanence and stability, a contrast to the transitory nature of human life, particularly that of a soldier.

*Soldiers of the King's Shropshire Light Infantry, parading in the Castle Green prior to embarkation to France in 1915.*

1. Letter of 1933 by Housman in reply to a questionnaire by M.M. Pollett.
2. *The Shropshire Lad* (1896): 3 ('The Recruit'), 7 ('When smoke blew up from Ludlow'), 23 ('The lads in their hundreds . . .'), 58 ('When I came last to Ludlow'), 62 ('Terence'); *Last Poems* (1922): 34 ('The First of May').
3. The Ludlow carillon has existed since 1638 or earlier but the present mechanism was installed in 1890. On Sundays the chimes play *Psalm 104* (Hanover).

The second poem quoted, called 'The First of May', was written about 1905 and first printed in *The Cambridge Review* in 1914. It later appeared as no.34 in *Last Poems* (1922). The poem reflects Housman's interest in nature but again the major contrast is between transitory human life on the one hand and recurring events on the other, the annual May Fair being a convenient example.[4] In the background, as always, is 'the sumless tale of sorrow'; but in a lighter vein the second verse catches exactly the carefree mood of generations of south Salopians, walking or riding to Ludlow Fair.

*The photograph above, by Thomas Jones, was taken from the fields between Sheet Road and what was later Steventon New Road, near the end of the modern Mary Elizabeth Road. The stile in the foreground and the luxuriant vegetation echo the mood of the poem while a gap in the trees affords a distant view of Ludlow tower.*

*This photograph, taken in 1906, shows a part of Ludlow fair close to the time when Housman wrote his poem. The young men in the foreground, wearing caps and Edwardian suits, are the sort with whom Housman identified himself in his poems. Stalls line Castle Street, just as they do today, but the modern Helter-Skelter is less solid and has been relegated to Mill Street.*

**The First of May**

The orchards half the way
From home to Ludlow fair
Flowered on the first of May
In Mays when I was there;
And seen from stile or turning
The plume of smoke would show,
Where fires were burning
That went out long ago.

The plum broke forth in green,
The pear stood high and snowed,
My friends and I between
Would take the Ludlow road;
Dressed to the nines and drinking
And light in heart and limb,
And each chap thinking
The fair was held for him.

Between the trees in flower
New friends at fairtime tread
The way where Ludlow tower
Stands planted on the dead.
Our thoughts, a long while after,
They think, our words they say;
Theirs now the laughter,
The fair, the first of May.

Ay, yonder lads are yet
The fools that we were then;
For oh, the sons we get
Are still the sons of men.
The sumless tale of sorrow
Is all unrolled in vain:
May comes to-morrow
And Ludlow fair again.

4. The right to hold a May Fair was one of the ancient privileges confirmed by the 1461 Charter of Incorporation. By 1552 it had been replaced by fairs later in the year and it was not revived until the mid-1820s. It became a fun fair in the mid 19th century and has always been held in the streets, in spite of periodic complaints by local tradesmen.

There was a postcard boom in the early decades of the 20th century, for postal charges were low and some other forms of communication, e.g. the telephone, were still expensive. While many postcards were comic or sentimental, topographical subjects were also very popular. Large firms such as Friths, Judges and Valentines operated on a nation-wide basis, producing series of local views. Local photographers also cashed in on the craze and were in a unique pos-ition to record local events which varied from commissioned set-pieces to catastrophes and accidents which had to be covered at very short notice.

Roll-film was very seldom used at this time by professional photographers and cards were almost always contact printed from much larger plate glass negatives and therefore often varied slightly in relation to the position of the plates.

This historic photograph was one of several taken by T. J. Evans of No. 5 Corve Street at the commissioning of the new Merryweather steam fire-engine on 15 October 1910 in Castle Square. In it can be seen the changes in nearly 200 years of fire fighting in Ludlow.

On the left is a manual pump by Richard Newsham of London which was presented to the Ludlow brigade in 1726 by Sir Littleton Powys in gratitude for assistance given at a fire at Henley Hall. On the right is the horse-drawn manual machine by Hadley, Simpkin and Co., bought by Ludlow Corporation in 1831, which could be taken quickly with its crew to areas well out of Ludlow. In the centre is the Merryweather *Greenwich Gem* steam pump, with 'Ludlow Fire Brigade' proudly inscribed. With this machine the brigade entered the 20th century and, at a dramatic public demonstration shortly after the photograph was taken, water was drawn out of the Teme at the bottom of Mill Street, pumped up the street through 1,300 ft. of hose and played onto the Market Hall roof, a vertical height of 125 ft.

The august helmeted figure on the right of the steamer is the brigade Captain, A.W. Packer; on the left is the Mayor, Councillor George Woodhouse; while in the centre is the Mayor's grandson who ceremonially lit the boiler.

A watery scene taken in 1924 in Lower Corve Street, at that time the main road out of Ludlow to Shrewsbury, when the River Corve burst its banks after a dramatic thunder storm. Before the bed of the Corve was lowered by dredging the property on the west side of the street was greatly neglected and the barrels in the cellar of the *Unicorn Inn* (on the left beyond the archway) were regularly awash in time of flood.

This is a part of the town of great historic interest. In the Middle Ages the land on the left was Dinmore Fee and the rents paid by tenants helped to support St Leonard's chapel (see p. 89). In later centuries this was an important leather-making district, dominated by families of tanners and glovers like the Powises and the Earsleys. In the 1920s miscellaneous businesses had their premises here. e.g. the signboards of Wait and Sons, bakers, and Davies and Sons, motor hauliers, can be seen at Nos. 70 (left) and 82 (right) respectively.

The view of Church Street (above left) was taken in the 1920s for J. C. Austen, then a printer in Castle Street. The cobbled surface remained until the 1940s. On the left is the sign board of Henry Tantrum, a baker who made white-cakes, Ludlow's best known home-made delicacy. Beyond, sporting a stag's head, is a late medieval shop, part of a complex built in 1492 round what is now the *Rose and Crown* courtyard. The buildings on the right, mostly 18th century, preserve the plan of the 13th-century Butchers' Row.

The Reader's House (above right) was one of the 'picturesque' timber framed houses which made the town popular with motorists in the 1920s and 1930s and was open to the public. The house got its name because it was the official residence of the Reader, one of the curates of the Parish Church, in the 18th century; but parts of it are medieval while the fine Jacobean porch was added to what was previously the back of the house in 1616 by the Chaplain to the Council of the Marches. The photograph is by W.A. Call of Monmouth and was taken c.1920.

Retailers often produced or commissioned postcards of their own premises which were given or sold to customers. This postcard of the early 1920s is of Sale and Higginson, ironmongers, of No. 148 Corve Street, the property which had once been the *Holy Lamb Inn*. Ironmongery was an important trade in a country market town, the window display reflecting the variety of goods which were stocked. On the left there are principally edge-tools, while the right hand window is filled with every shape and size of paraffin lamp, reminding us that very few country homes would have had electricity at this time although the town had been lit by gas for over a century. In the street we see rush-baskets, sickles, broom heads, doormats, and a wooden yoke for milking. Of the three gentlemen standing in the door, the figure on the right is Fred Northover who was a well-known Ludlow character.

As photographic processes became simpler and the cost of a camera less, more amateurs took up photography as a hobby. They recorded parts of the town neglected by the professionals and the albums which they lovingly assembled, often lying neglected in attics or deep cupboards, are exciting sources of information. One of the best photographers in Ludlow was Jane Green (1864-1936), a single lady of private means, who lived at No.145 Corve Street, a property still owned by members of her family. Two of her photographs are among those reproduced below.

*A rare view of Linney in the north-west of the ancient borough, looking towards the River Corve. Until the post 1945 period there was little settlement here, probably due to the risk of flooding, but the area was burgaged by the 13th century. The original rectilinear grid plan is still discernible, though by the 16th century many properties had been amalgamated to form small enclosed fields known as closes. The original burgage width was 66 ft. and one such property can still be seen, running back from the road behind the house now called Linney Fields. In the 19th century most of this area was used for pasture but the ridge and furrow in the foreground of the picture testifies to former cultivation.*

*(Above left) This photograph by Jane Green shows the eastern end of Tower Street in the 1890s. It is dominated by the Gaol, the grim stone building on the right, which was designed in the 1760s by T.F. Pritchard. It occupied part of the site of Galdeford Tower and Gateway, which had spanned the street since the 13th century. It became a Police Station in the 1880s and the Superintendant occupied the Victorian house next door.*

*(Above centre) This picture, behind what is now No.139 Corve Street, is one of several taken by Jane Green which show living conditions in the poorer parts of the town. The timber-framed building fronts the street while the white-washed brick building and the narrow alley run back down the medieval burgage plot. The census returns of 1881 show that several households were often crammed into such properties, where sanitation was often defective.*

*(Above right) A view of the property on the corner of Old Street and Tower Street, taken just before it ceased to be the Pheasant Inn in 1910. The photograph was taken by a relative of Thomas Sheldon, the last licensee. The building has late medieval features and had been inherited from the Palmers' Guild by the Corporation, who leased it to tenants for £1 p.a. It was later a grocer's shop and is now an Indian restaurant.*

William St John Hope (1854-1919) was a distinguished historian who served for many years as assistant secretary to the Society of Antiquaries.[1] His work on Ludlow Castle, presented to the Society in 1908, remains the most authoritative study of the Castle yet made and has been frequently cited on previous pages. It was based on excavations carried out during the summers of 1903-7 and it was during these periods in Ludlow that he formulated his ideas about the town plan. These were presented to the Society in 1909 in what is now regarded as a seminal paper on medieval planned towns, 'The Ancient Topography of the Town of Ludlow'.[2]

St John Hope was the first historian to draw attention to 'the marked regularity' of Ludlow's streets and to deduce that Ludlow was 'a planned town' with 'a deliberate attempt at symmetrical arrangement'. He draws attention to:

1. The partly filled in east-west High Street:

   *There can be little doubt . . . that the principal or High Street was a broad thoroughfare extending east and west along the high ground up to the castle gatehouse, now represented by King Street, High Street, Castle Street and Castle Square. But its eastern end has been considerably narrowed, and its western part encroached upon by later blocks of buildings, including the lately rebuilt Town Hall.*

2. Three main thoroughfares to the south with redundant streets east of Broad Street and west of Mill Street. Of the latter he writes:

   *. . . a curious strip of ground extending north and south, with gardens abutting on it east and west. This strip, which itself is now cut up into gardens, is strongly suggestive of having been laid down as one of the original streets of the town . . .*[3]

3. He postulates that the above 'strip' and other streets were 'curtailed' when the outer bailey of the Castle was built in the late 12th century:

   *In my paper on Ludlow Castle it was pointed out that there were reasons for thinking that the outer bailey was an addition to the original plan, made nearly a century later than the first building of the Castle. Now before this outer bailey was added, the High Street in all probability continued westward, so as to lead directly to the Castle entrance, and the street under notice no doubt extended northward to meet it. Such an arrangement would practically have reproduced that existing at the east end of the town, and had there been a cross street in continuation of Brand Lane and Bell Lane, debouching upon St Thomas's Chapel and Dinham Gate, the whole plan would have been so symmetrical that it is difficult to suppose it was not so originally . . .*

More recent work, especially by Conzen (1968), has caused some of Hope's conclusions to be amended; but his main thesis, that Ludlow was a planned town, remains unchallenged and is the starting point for all serious work on the town's physical growth.

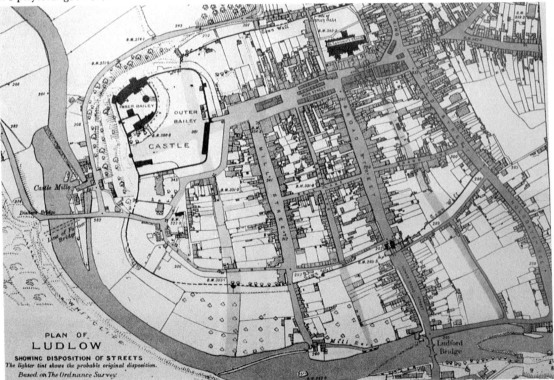

*The map of the central part of Ludlow which accompanied the article written by St John Hope. It has now been shown that the town plan extended further north incorporating areas adjoining Corve Street and Linney.*

1. *D.N.B.*
2. St John Hope, 1909.
3. It is now established that this strip was called Christ Croft.

The 20th century brought a deluge of topographical books and travel guides, many of which are eulogistic about Ludlow. Especially after World War II a few perceptive writers have drawn attention to the limitation of such books. E.B. Musman, for instance, wrote in 1948: *For its size Ludlow receives from the compilers of guidebooks as much attention as any town in England . . . but . . . only occasionally, by writers like Mr. Christopher Hussey, is the architectural sequence noted and emphasised . . .*[1]

Christopher Hussey (1899-1970) was a distinguished architectural critic and historian, who contributed to *Country Life* for 50 years and was its editor from 1933 to 1940.[2] He wrote four articles on Ludlow, which were carefully researched in 1943[3] and were published in 1945 and 1946 in *Country Life.*[4] They are among the best pieces of writing yet done on Ludlow, though surprisingly Corve Street is almost completely ignored. In the third of these articles, he expands on the theme of architectural sequence: *By architectural sequence is meant not only historic continuity of building but the visual effect produced by that continuity: the quality appealing to both eye and mind in a group of buildings of many ages yet comprising a whole that is strangely satisfying. This is an aspect of town architecture not generally dealt with by guide and text books that note historic events and outstanding buildings individually. But it is the aspect most sought by the connoisseur of townscape . . .* A little further on this approach is applied to Ludlow: *The importance of such a place as Ludlow, which ought to be a National Monument, in its entirety, is that it is still virtually intact besides being exceptional in site and history. Owing to its great richness in this matter of architectural sequence the art of building from the Conquest to 1840 can be studied better than perhaps in any one place in England.*

This photograph shows a range of buildings on the west side of Old Street, photographed in the early 1950s, which illustrate Hussey's 'architectural continuity'. On the left is No.10, rebuilt by the Corporation in 1622 as the Preacher's House. At No.12, early 20th century pebble-dash and mock timber framing mask an older structure. No. 10 now the Shropshire County Library, had a Regency front put on when it was the Golden Lion, an important inn. Hussey draws attention to the arcading, here used to economise wall thickness. Further up the street, the tall gables of the old Prince Rupert Inn, built in the 17th century, and the Tolsey, built c.1420, are still rendered with plaster but they provide a prominent and pleasing end to the sequence, while the view is 'closed in' by the irregular shape of the Bull Ring.

This photograph shows an architectural sequence noted by Hussey. The six-bay facade of the Guildhall was erected in 1768, to the design of Thomas Farnolls Pritchard (see p.71); but it masks a 15th century timber-framed building which was the headquarters of the Palmers' Guild (see p.26). This building was an aisled hall, the only one known in Shropshire. The three-storey houses to the right, built in 1713, occupy part of the former Guildhall enclosure. On the far right is the Blue Boar Inn, a late 17th century building which was once called the Portcullis because of its proximity to the enclosure gateway. The smaller buildings on the left occupy two of the strips into which some Palmers' Guild property was divided. A timber-framed cottage is clad in weather boarding, rarely found locally.

1. In Cumberledge,S., *Recording Britain*, Vol.3 (1948), p.64.
2. *D.N.B.*
3. Letters in papers of Thomas Midgely (d.1950), now in possession of L.H.R.G.
4. *Country Life*, 21 Dec. 1945, pp.1084-97; 28 Dec. 1945, pp.1140-2; 8 Feb. 1946, pp.256-9; 15 Feb. 1946, pp.302-5.

# PART OF THE LUDLOW TOWNSCAPE, 1982

This oblique view of south east Ludlow, taken from the tower of the Parish Church in 1982, illustrates the complexity of townscape. Ludlow, like other historic towns, is a palimpsest of many centuries and even the most modern buildings are of interest to the urban historian, for they often preserve the shape of medieval properties. This part of the town was neglected by 18th and 19th century tourists and has rarely featured in the preceeding pages of this book; but it has always been of great economic importance and the town's two largest factories are situated here today.

The line of the **Bull Ring** and **Old Street**, running diagonally across the picture from the bottom left hand corner, preserves the course of the north-south prehistoric routeway through the Welsh Marches. In the foreground the timber framed **Tolsey**, restored by the Civic Society in 1965, occupies an island site in the triangular **'Beaste Market'**. To the right is an imposing range of 16th and 17th century timber-framed buildings, occupying 22 ft. wide plots which colonised the original wide market place in the late 13th century. Some of the properties on the far side of Old Street are even earlier e.g. the **courtyard complex** on the corner, parts of which are now an Indian restaurant. David Lloyd, one of the authors of this book, lived here until he was 17. Further down Old Street crowded properties were demolished in the 1930s to accommodate the **Clifton Cinema**, which is now a Bingo Hall; but beyond is a classic example of back building along a burgage plot, where the town's first **Primitive Methodist chapel**, built in 1837, reaches to the town wall. A new chapel, built in 1871, can be seen to the right. It is part of the premises of **E.Walters Ltd.**, clothing manufacturers, who came to Ludlow in 1957 and now have 285 employees. They have expanded into modern buildings beyond the town wall and two of the narrow burgage plots fronting onto Lower Galdeford have been acquired for access.

The narrow **Tower Street**, once called 'Galdeford within the Gate', can be seen running east from the Bull Ring. Beyond the line of the town wall, where Galdeford Tower once stood (see p.85), the street widens at a Y shaped junction, with **Upper Galdeford** to the left and **Lower Galdeford** to the right. In the middle distance, to the right of Lower Galdeford, can be seen the extensive premises of **F.W.McConnell Ltd.**, who came to Ludlow in 1947 and make agricultural machinery. Their oldest buildings were erected as a 'food dump' in the Second World War. Beyond are modern **housing estates** but the **Ludlow-Hereford railway** can also be seen, following a route engineered by migrant navvies in 1852-3. The sloping ground behind the railway was once part of **Waretree Field**, one of the town's largest open fields which took its name from the 'Waretree' or gallows which stood on the crest of the hill, more or less in line with Lower Galdeford. The modern by-pass is hidden beyond the crest but the conical hill crowned by the Iron Age **Caynham Camp** can be seen in the centre of the picture while to the left is the long southern slope of **Titterstone Clee Hill**.

The group was formed in September 1976 to study all aspects of the history of Ludlow. The first objectives were to reconstruct the tenurial history of all Ludlow properties and to study the architecture of standing buildings. The results of this research are now being used for studies of the town's economic, social and architectural history.

The observer is looking west. These properties abut onto St Laurence's churchyard.

rebuilt 1905　　　　　　thick stone walls　　　　　　curved wind-braces at rear c.1500

| Modern street number | 9 | 10 | 11 | 12 | 13 |
|---|---|---|---|---|---|
| Earliest known reference | c.1330: Palmers' Guild; house and shop leased to Nyechus Ferror, smith | | c.1270: Wenlock Priory; leased to Wm. Moyle | 1319: Isold d. of Henry le Swerdslipere to Richard de Corve: all that tenement I have from her father (except 2 solars under 1 roof and a lantern at end of tenement next to graveyard)—this building was on the site of the present Reader's House. | |
| 1482 Owner | Palmers' Guild | | Palmers' Guild (to Wenlock Priory) | Palmers' Guild (Scholehouse at rear) | |
| Leaseholder | John Ferrar, blacksmith tenement & workshop (20s) | | William Adyns tenement (8s) | ap Gogh, tailor tenement (18s) | |
| 1669 Owner | Corporation | | Corporation | Corporation | |
| Leaseholder | Philip Jones, mercer (13s 4d) | | Mrs. Fletcher (10s) | Mrs. Fletcher (16s 8d) | |
| 1667 Head | Richard Taylor | | Edward Hunt | John Lewis | |
| Occupation | tailor | | corviser | chandler | |
| Wife | 1 | | 1 | 1 | |
| Other adults | 0 | | 0 | 0 | |
| Children | 2 | | 2 | 1 | |
| Svts./Apps. | 0 | | 2 | 0 | |
| Total | 4 | | 6 | 3 | |
| 1672 Hearths | 2 | | 1 | 7 | |
| 1841 Head | Mrs. Minton | John Evans | William Smith | James Jones | George Griffiths |
| Occupation | fishmonger | shoemaker | grocer | saddler | farmer |
| Wife | 0 | 1 | 0 | 1 | 1 |
| Other adults | 0 | 0 | 0 | 0 | 0 |
| Children (ages) | 0 | 5 (3-14) | 0 | 1 (1) | 0 |
| Svts. | 1 | 0 | 2 | 2 | 1 |
| Assts./Apps. | 0 | 0 | 2 | 0 | 0 |
| Total | 2 | 7 | 5 | 4 | 3 |
| 1843 Owner | Borough Council | Borough Council | Borough Council | Borough Council | Borough Council |
| Leaseholder | S. Dayos, butcher (6s 8d) | Wm. Smith, grocer (6s 8d) | William Smith grocer (10s) | James Jones, saddler (8s 4d) | George Griffiths, farmer (8s 4d) |
| 1980 Occupant | Midland Bank | | C. Jones, butcher | Winter Gardens | City of Rome (clothes) |

**Sources of information on specified years.**
**Earliest known reference:** early Palmers' Guild rentals, e.g. 1270 (SRO 1996/16/1); early Palmers' Guild title deeds (SRO 356 MTI - 1442).
**1482:** Corporation burgage roll (SRO 356 box 400); Palmers' Guild rental (ibid, box 322).
**1669:** Corporation burgage rental (SRO 356 box 400).

The visual summary below is part of an exhibition on the Bull Ring presented for Ludlow Festival in 1980. The details given are for years when particularly good documentation is available for the whole town but much more information has been discovered about each property. This part of the Bull Ring was referred to as part of Corve Street in the Middle Ages.

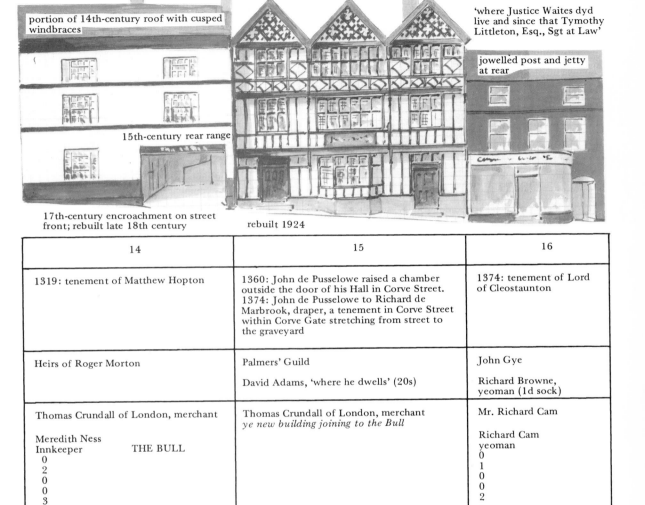

portion of 14th-century roof with cusped windbraces

'where Justice Waites dyd live and since that Tymothy Littleton, Esq., Sgt at Law'

jowelled post and jetty at rear

15th-century rear range

17th-century encroachment on street front; rebuilt late 18th century

rebuilt 1924

| 14 | 15 | 16 |
|---|---|---|
| 1319: tenement of Matthew Hopton | 1360: John de Pusselowe raised a chamber outside the door of his Hall in Corve Street.<br>1374: John de Pusselowe to Richard de Marbrook, draper, a tenement in Corve Street within Corve Gate stretching from street to the graveyard | 1374: tenement of Lord of Cleostaunton |
| Heirs of Roger Morton | Palmers' Guild<br><br>David Adams, 'where he dwells' (20s) | John Gye<br><br>Richard Browne, yeoman (1d sock) |
| Thomas Crundall of London, merchant<br><br>Meredith Ness<br>Innkeeper     THE BULL<br>0<br>2<br>0<br>0<br>3<br>12 | Thomas Crundall of London, merchant<br>*ye new building joining to the Bull*<br><br><br><br><br><br><br>3 | Mr. Richard Cam<br><br>Richard Cam<br>yeoman<br>0<br>1<br>0<br>0<br>2<br>4 |
| William Pea<br>publican     THE BULL<br>1<br>0<br>0<br>4<br>0<br>6<br>William Pea, publican | Arthur Evans<br>publican     THE ELEPHANT AND CASTLE<br>1<br>3<br>2 (1-2)<br>2<br>0<br>9<br>Borough Council<br>William Jennings (20s) . | Thomas Bowen<br>cabinet maker<br>1<br>0<br>0<br>1<br>0<br>3<br>Mrs. Pryce |
| The Bull Hotel | National Provincial Bank | Capitol Carpets |

**1667:** Faraday,M.A., 'The Ludlow Poll Tax Returns of 1667', *T.S.A.S.*, vol.59 (1971-2), pp.104-23.
**1672:** Watkins-Pritchard,W., *The Shropshire Hearth Roll of 1672* (1949), pp.162-7.
**1841:** Census returns.
**1843:** Ludlow Borough Rate Book (SRO 1996).

*(Drawings by Stanley Woolston, Ludlow)*

| | |
|---|---|
| Baker | Baker, O., *Ludlow Town and Neighbourhood* (3rd ed., 1906) |
| B.L. | British Library |
| Bryan | Bryan, *Dictionary of Painters and Engravers* (4th ed., 1903-4) |
| Burne | Burne, C. S., *Shropshire Folk Lore* (1883) |
| Clayton | Clayton, J., *Timber Framed Edifices of the West Midlands* (1846) |
| Conzen | Conzen, M. R. G., 'The use of town plans in the study of urban history' in Deyos, H. J. (ed.), *The Study of Urban History* (1968), pp. 124-6 |
| Cranage | Cranage, D. H. S., *An Architectural Account of the Churches of Shropshire*, part 2, *The Hundred of Munswell* (1895) |
| *D.N.B.* | *Dictionary of National Biography* |
| Eyton | Eyton, R. W., *Antiquities of Shropshire*, vol. 5 (1861) |
| Foster | Foster, J., *Alumni Oxoniensis*, 8 vols. (1891) |
| Ganderton and Lafond | Ganderton, A. W. and Lafond, J., *Ludlow Stained and Painted Glass* (1961) |
| Grant | Grant, M. H., *A Dictionary of British Landscape Painters* (1952) |
| H.R.O. | Herefordshire County Record Office |
| Jukes | Jukes, T. F. (ed.), *Edward Lloyd: Antiquities of Shropshire* (1844) |
| Lloyd, 1977 | Lloyd, D. J., *Country Grammar School* (1977) |
| Lloyd, 1979 | Lloyd, D. J., *Broad Street* (Ludlow Research Paper No. 3, 1979) |
| L.H.R.G. | Ludlow Historical Research Group |
| *L.P.R.* | *Ludlow Parish Register, 1558-1813* |
| Moir | Moir, A. L., *Historic Ludlow Castle and those associated with it* (1960) |
| M.T. | Muniment of Title |
| Pevsner | Pevsner, Sir N., *Shropshire* (Buildings of England series, 1958) |
| P.R.O. | Public Record Office |
| *R.S.* | *Rolls Series* |
| St John Hope, 1908 | St John Hope, W. H., 'The Castle of Ludlow', *Archaeologia*, vol. 61, part 1, pp. 257-238 |
| St John Hope, 1909 | St John Hope, W. H., 'The Ancient Topography of the Town of Ludlow', *Archaeologia*, vol. 61, part 2, pp. 383-8 |
| S.R.O. | Shropshire County Record Office |
| Speight and Lloyd | Speight, Dr. M. E. and Lloyd, D. J., *Ludlow Houses and their Residents* (Ludlow Research Paper No. 1, 1978) |
| *T.W.N.F.C.* | *Transactions of the Woolhope Naturalists' Field Club* (Herefordshire) |
| *T.S.A.S.* | *Transactions of the Shropshire Archaeological Society* |
| Vaughan | Vaughan, J., *The English Guide Book*, *c.*1780-1870 (1974) |
| *V.C.H.* | *Victoria County History* |
| Weyman, 1895 | Weyman, H. T., 'The Members of Parliament for Ludlow', *T.S.A.S.*, ser. 2, vol. 8 (1895), p. 1-54 |
| Weyman, 1911 | Weyman, H. T., *Royal Visits to Ludlow* (1911) |
| Weyman, 1913 | Weyman, H. T., *Ludlow in Bye-Gone Days* (1913) |
| Weyman, 1925 | Weyman, H. T., *The Glass in Ludlow Church* (2nd ed., 1925) |
| Wightman | Wightman, W. E., *The Lacy Family in England and Normandy, 1066-1194* (1966) |
| Williams | Williams, P., *The Council of the Marches of Wales under Elizabeth the First* (1958) |
| Wright, 1852 | Wright, T., *The History of Ludlow* (1852) |
| Wright, 1867 | Wright, T., *Ludlow Sketches* (1867) |